NOT the
Perfect
Church

Sue Weller

DAY THREE EDITIONS
an imprint of Maritime Books

Not The Perfect Church

First published 2009

First edition

Copyright © Sue Weller, 2009
The moral right of the author has been asserted

Published by Day Three Editions
an imprint of Maritime Books
Lodge Hill
Liskeard
PL14 4EL
UK

Printed in England by CPI Bookmarque Ltd, Croydon

ISBN 978-1-904459-39-2

Sue Weller is a writer and artist living in Falmouth, Cornwall

Also by Sue Weller...

Me and My Bleeding Mouth
the painful true story of Gary McCormick

This book is dedicated to my children,
Zoe and Tom and Toby,
who inspire me,
each in their own very individual way.

Contents

PASTORAL LETTERS

John Gillespie's letters to his church family

Then Jesus came to them and said,
'All authority in heaven
and on earth has been given to me.
Therefore go and make disciples of all nations,
baptising them in the name of the Father
and of the Son and of the Holy Spirit,
and teaching them to obey everything
I have commanded you.
And surely I am with you always,
to the very end of the age.'
Matthew 28:19-20

PUBLISHER'S NOTE

Some of the content of this book will seem surprisingly revealing, especially for a church! But by being candid about what has happened in our fellowship and by writing it down for publication we hope that churches elsewhere may gain from what we have experienced – and eventually be encouraged.

We went through tough times but God has been in control throughout.

As this book goes to print it is fourteen years since Grace Community Church began, so the passing of time may have blurred some of the details of timing of events. The story is recounted by three people who were with the church when it began; we apologise if any of the facts that follow do not match exactly those in the memories of others who were involved during that exciting time.

THANKS...

When I was asked to put into words the story of Grace Community Church I had to decide whose voices to use. This was a difficult decision, as I knew that everyone who had been involved from the beginning would have his or her own story. I had to narrow it down to a handful of characters and I apologise to all those loyal and dedicated people who have not been named in this book; thankfully, God knows who you are!

Thank you to John Gillespie for trusting me with this venture; to Angie Godfrey, Jan Jones and Lyn Salvage for praying for me throughout the project; and to Lynn Critchley, Tessa Gillespie and Rose Pollard for their gracious hospitality during my sorties to Morval and Liskeard.

Sue Weller
Falmouth

PART ONE

THE END OF A DREAM

What lies behind the creation of a church?

What are the struggles, the sacrifices, the lessons learned through pain and joy?

This is the story of one church that had its beginnings in heartache and loss.

John Gillespie is the pastor of Grace Community Church, at Morval, a hamlet near Looe on the south Cornwall coast.

He begins our narrative...

1

Beginnings

It was never my intention to talk about myself in this book. This is God's story, not mine, and I've never wanted the focus to be on me; after all, if I hadn't been willing to follow the Lord He would have used someone else.

But I do want people to share the excitement of knowing what it is like to trust God when you are faced with what seems to be the end of your dreams, and when what lies ahead appears to be an impossible situation. Trusting God in all circumstances isn't easy but, to me, that seems to be what the story of the Grace Community Church family is all about. And, as the story of our church is to be told I suppose it might as well start with me! Bear with me as I turn the clock back quite a few years, to give you some background.

I was one of three children born to John and Martha Gillespie in Rochester, a large city on the shore of Lake Ontario across the lake from Toronto, in upstate New York in the United States. My family had been Methodists for generations, harkening back to rural days in Arkansas where preachers rode horses from church to church and lived rough.

My father held many of the positions that a layman can hold in the United Methodist Church, everything from Sunday school teacher to chairman of the Church Board. A son of the Depression, raised in absolute poverty in the dustbowl years in South Arkansas, he worked as a businessman in the photographic industry. My mother came from a completely different background; she was the only child of a Wall Street stockbroker. They met during World War II at university in Missouri and were married just before my father left for Europe and the war, where he was a navigator in the USAAF (the United States Army Air Force).

In our family we were encouraged to work hard and play hard; I loved sport – I began golf at the age of four and played American football through high school. My parents being children of the Depression and devout Methodists knew how to work hard and how to work with integrity. They wouldn't compromise principles.

I spent the first eight years of my life overseas in the Philippines and Brazil; my father was in international business so it seemed that an awareness of the whole world was just something my siblings and I grew up with. We were around international people all the time when I was a youngster and our home was regularly filled with people from all over the world to do with my father's business.

I became a committed churchgoer but not a committed Christian. Our church was very liberal in theology so I did not hear the gospel clearly presented. I didn't understand the wonders of God's grace; I just thought it was about trying to be good and hoping for the best. My life revolved around American football and golf.

In 1975, at the age of eighteen, I left Rochester to go to university in Ohio, to study business law. Coming from my background I couldn't imagine doing anything else. My aim was to make a lot of money as a businessman or as a lawyer in some sort of field or industry.

At university I met believing evangelical Christians who were not at all like the churchgoers I had grown up with. There was something about them that immediately attracted me to them… their heart, their lifestyle, their loving aggression for the Lord. I think I was probably a very obnoxious eighteen-year-old, pretty full of my own opinions, outspoken and hard to teach, and yet they had a great love for me and tolerated my many shortcomings. Most of them were only a couple of

11

years older than me; a few were my age, but they seemed wise beyond their years. More than anything I saw that they had a real zeal for the Lord – a living faith. I had never seen Christians love God as these folk did.

Our campus fellowship, under the leadership of our pastor Bruce Montgomery, met regularly for Bible study and fellowship. The most exciting meetings were Tuesday nights when about two hundred and fifty of us would convene in a university cafeteria. Bruce would teach the Bible in a real way, like he really meant it, and the singing was lively and modern. The fellowship we had among us was genuine and life changing. We also established numerous sports teams that competed aggressively on campus and in so doing were a really good witness for Christ.

It was some time during my first year at university that I came to trust Jesus Christ truly as my Saviour. I can't say that I remember the exact moment – mine wasn't an emotional conversion, but nevertheless it was very real. I worked through all the standard reading material: Josh McDowell's Evidence That Demands A Verdict, More Than A Carpenter; John Stott's Basic Christianity; the writings of C S Lewis and Francis Schaeffer... all this convinced me of the historical truth of the Gospel and began to arm my mind for battles ahead.

Over the months I came to a convinced belief that Jesus Christ was indeed the Son of God. Christ, and the scriptures, came alive to me, and even at this early stage in my new faith I began to realise that the Bible was really true. I was aware that I was breaking free from the crumbling moorings of the liberalism I had grown up with. I couldn't see how else to walk with God if I couldn't accept the Bible as the truth; if I were to begin to play cut and paste with the Bible where would it end? Surely that would be dangerous? I also began to realise that because my upbringing had been very liberal theologically I had never heard a clear presentation of the Gospel.

(I'm assuming here that everyone understands the difference between liberal and evangelical, but I would like to define what the words mean to me. My view is that an evangelical takes the Bible to be the inspired, authoritative and sufficient Word of God, a divine book; a liberal believes the Bible to be a book of human origins containing perhaps true, perhaps false, sentiments about God.)

Over the next three years I studied for and completed my business law degree; at the same time I became increasingly involved in the Christian campus fellowship. I had a great hunger for the Bible and began to preach and to teach in little ways, at our Christian fellowship meetings and occasionally as one of a group in a local church. Some of my early forays into both preaching and teaching were pretty miserable (I believe, all these years later, that some of my current forays are pretty miserable), but God had planted a lot of patient people around me. The core values of our fellowship were simple; Christ-centred, Bible-based and people-loving. Looking back now I think wow, what a wonderful place to learn Christ.

Increasingly I began to feel called into a life of Christian ministry. I never heard a voice, I never saw a vision regarding it, there was just an inward conviction that I was to spend my life vocationally for Christ. I suppressed it for a year or two while continuing at university but, just previous to graduating with my business law degree, I surrendered to what I believe to be a call to vocational ministry.

Another very special thing happened to me while I was at university; I met Tessa, who was to become my wife. She was studying art education and I saw her for the first time at one of the Christian Fellowship meetings. She was a noble-minded, forthright young woman and almost from the first time I saw her I was very attracted to her. She had so many outstanding qualities but most notably a determined spirit and a passionate commitment to following Jesus Christ.

We began courting but by then I had decided to go to theology school in Texas and in my folly I ended the relationship abruptly and made preparations to move to Southern Methodist University in Dallas. Tessa was heart-broken, as she steadfastly believed we were right for each other.

In 1979 I left university and the interdenominational fellowship where I had been loved and nurtured in my first taste of a relationship

13

with a living Lord Jesus, and went to Perkins School of Theology at the Southern Methodist University in Dallas. Convinced that I was going to change the world I was very excited about the prospects of what lay ahead. There was no doubt in my mind that I would become a Methodist minister.

2

The Frustrating Years

Having been raised in the United Methodist Church and then coming to Christ in an evangelical fellowship I was passionate about Methodism because it's what I knew, it's what my family knew. I was in awe of John Wesley, his ardour for the Gospel, his love for truth, his zeal for evangelism.

I spent four years in Dallas, where in the midst of theological liberalism I remained convinced the Bible was the inspired Word of God. I made some great friends there and we supported each other in our academic battles for truth.

Because by and large the school was very liberal theologically there were many issues I disagreed with. Was Jesus Christ really the Son of God? Did He really rise from the dead? Was the Bible truly God-breathed, sufficient and authoritative? These were questions that, to me, had obvious answers that were to be found in the Bible.

I'm afraid I was a bit of a nuisance at theology school. I didn't set out to be, but because I was convinced of certain truths I often questioned my teachers. They seemed to interpret the Bible according to their own beliefs; I was disturbed by this and determined to put across my point of view. I was often quite agitated and couldn't keep quiet when my convictions collided with my professors' teachings. I came to believe that liberalism was basically a form of humanism with religious words attached to it.

The crux of the matter was this: is the Bible a divinely inspired book or not?

It seemed as though many of my professors assumed it to be human musings about God; I believed this to be insufficient, unfaithful to historic Christianity and poisonous to true faith.

My opinions were not so much my own as reflective of my evangelical heritage and historic Methodism. I was convinced of the foundations of the Christian faith and I believed that they were being questioned at theology school. I saw many students who, it seemed to me, were just theologically confused. I saw professors who contributed to their confusion, and these students were going out into the ministry, taking with them their own liberal views of the Word of God. It didn't seem right to me, whichever way I looked at it.

Looking back now, with the benefit of maturity (I hope!) it seems that the Word of God was planted in me at the point of my conversion and that I saw it differently from the very beginning. I simply couldn't agree with my professors any more than I could, say, stop breathing, even though they had years and years of experience in studying the Bible. I probably came across as arrogant, or at least very intense, but it was the only way I could be. I was determined to be true to God and to historic Christianity and I didn't feel I was doing anything new.

I think philosophically I was what I would call an evidentialist. I believed in the historical evidence for the Christian faith, and I was convinced of the historical reliability of the scriptures and of the whole Christ event, and I remain so to this day. Of course, I went to theology school with plenty to learn, but I wasn't confused about what I really believed; I was clear about the Christian faith and my position in it.

So my years at theology school were pretty frustrating really. There was plenty of fun, plenty of sports, lots of music, I played in rock and roll bands, and made the most of all the best that the Lone Star State had to offer, but as far as my faith was concerned it was a pretty frustrating time, except for one year that, in complete contrast, was perhaps the most marvellous year of my life.

I was given the opportunity to pastor two small churches in rural Arkansas as an internship. I preached three times a week and had plenty of time to pastor the people. It was just way out in the countryside; each church had a congregation of about thirty people, and I spent the year preaching, hunting and fishing, as well as feasting on the country fare that seemed to accompany every pastoral visit! It was just an idyllic year for a young man. I was twenty-four.

· ∞ ·

In January 1982, while I was seconded to Arkansas, I was praying and asking the Lord specifically what should be the next step in my life after my last year at theology school, and the Lord most clearly spoke to my heart that, after nearly four years of ducking and diving, I was to make contact again with Tessa.

She had coped so well with the time we were apart. God had sustained her and because she knew I was the right one for her she had diligently waited and prayed for me during the four years of our separation. Within a month she flew down from Ohio to Arkansas to see me. Two days later we drove to my parents' home (they had retired to the mountains of Arkansas) and after only one day with my parents my dad said to me, 'If you let this girl go without a ring on her finger, you're crazy.' We were engaged the next day and married in June of that year. She knew that the Lord had brought us together four years earlier and her steadfastness and determination to wait for me had won the day. (Tessa says, quite rightly, that the Lord was in control and knew that the timing four years earlier was not right. He won the day! Praise Him!) I could write a whole book about Tessa, she's so important to me, but I had better keep on track…

The Perkins School of Theology had a system whereby they would send students for one year to fill in gaps in British Methodist churches, so when I graduated in 1983 Tessa and I went to the UK with our first child, Bethany, in our arms. We both felt without doubt that we were called to do this and the Lord arranged that we went to Kidsgrove in Stoke-on-Trent for a year.

17

We had a wonderful year. What do I mean by wonderful? Well, we just preached Christ and loved the people; it was so uncomplicated and the people welcomed us with open arms. We were still only kids as far as ministry was concerned, with everything to learn, so we weren't there to change policies and to formulate the future and all that; we were there simply to love the people and to preach Christ. Those were our duties and it was a joy to do that.

In 1984 we returned to the States, to pastor three small churches in rural Arkansas and we spent three very frustrating years there. I had said boldly to the District Superintendent, 'Send me where no-one else wants to go.' The trouble was that within days of arriving back we realised that we were called to be in England, that we really should be back where we had just come from! Nevertheless we fulfilled three years of ministry in the States, though by and large I felt as if my pastoral services were unwanted by much of the church who seemed dull to truth and while we saw the Gospel have a precious impact on a number of lives, many there did not appreciate our ministry.

This feeling that we should be back in England hadn't suddenly appeared; we had felt it when we were in England, but just didn't have the courage to abide by it. Tessa is stronger than me, more resilient; she would have followed the feeling and stayed, but I had been homesick, just plain and simple homesick, needing to get back to the States. I just didn't have the courage to stay.

So although the three years spent back in the States felt frustrating, looking back I suppose that they were constructive because they were years in which, because of most of the people's lack of interest in Bible study, prayer meetings and door-to-door evangelism and those things which should occupy much of a pastor's time, I found myself with quite a bit of precious seclusion. I just studied and prayed, studied and prayed some more. The Lord gave me those years, I think, to enable me to make sure about where I stood theologically. With what lay ahead God knew that I would need that grounding.

Two wonderful events happened during that time: one is that my wife and I were blessed with the birth of our first two sons, Johnny and Jachin; the other is that I met weekly with the local Baptist and Assemblies of God pastors and we prayed long and hard for revival in that town. The Lord did move abundantly in answer to our prayer and we saw many people within the Baptist Church accept the Lord into their lives.

• ∞ •

As the months passed and the seasons came and went in Arkansas, we went about our duties as best as we possibly could, but Tessa and I had a relentless weight on our heart about the United Kingdom, about coming back to work here, and it just wouldn't go away. John Wesley said, 'Go where you're needed, but go where you're needed most.' I could see that the Christian scene in Europe was severely declined, more so than anywhere in the world, so I felt really burdened to be in England. We didn't have a sign from God… it would have been easier if we had, quite frankly, but there was nothing like that. There was just a continuous conviction that what little strength we had was to be given in England and not in the States.

During our time in Arkansas we began to explore ways to come back to the United Kingdom and I heard about an Englishman called Vic Jacobson who was preaching in Dallas, Texas. I felt that maybe he would have an answer for me, so I flew down to see him, asked his advice, and he said, 'If your connections are with Methodism make yourself available to the Methodist Church in England and go back.'

It sounded straightforward enough. First of all I checked with my Bishop; he approved and I wrote the Methodist Church a letter, asking them to receive me as an American Minister on loan, as it were. Tessa and I agreed that we'd go anywhere in the UK, we didn't mind where we ended up, and we told them that.

The day my letter arrived at Methodist Headquarters in England, offering myself, a letter from a circuit (a group of churches pastored by one minister) called Liskeard and Looe arrived on the same desk, saying that they needed a minister. Donald English, whose desk it was, checked us out through mutual contacts and phoned us to say we would be getting a letter from the circuit in Cornwall. We waited all day, the next day and were still waiting a week later when we were phoned again to be told that they wanted to pray over it for another week! We thought that was a good sign and of course we had been praying about it for the entire week! We looked at the atlas and found that the two places were on the south Cornwall coast.

Finally we received a telephone call from the then circuit steward of the Liskeard and Looe circuit, George Huddy, extending an invitation for me to serve as a circuit pastor for an initial period of three years. We had no idea what to expect but that didn't matter, we were just thrilled to be returning to England at last.

3

To England, To Stay

We spent the beginning of 1987 planning our return to England. Our desire was to come with absolute notions that the Gospel, the message of Christ crucified and resurrected, could answer any situation that we were going to encounter there. It was completely our desire to faithfully serve in the Methodist circuit in Liskeard and Looe. Yes, that was our total 100% desire!

By now our children were aged four, three and one and a half so planning a transatlantic move was a bit more difficult than planning, say, a Sunday School outing. Tessa oversaw the packing of our household; we sold or gave away most of our goods and flew on August 24th from Houston, Texas, to Gatwick, London, arriving on the morning of the next day.

We were greeted at Gatwick airport by George Huddy and another circuit steward called Henry Orton. Somehow we hadn't worked out the geography and had failed to realise that a six-hour car journey awaited us. Having just completed a transatlantic flight with three small children in arms we arrived in Looe much later that day absolutely exhausted.

Looe is a small, bustling tourist and fishing port of around 5,000 inhabitants. We were taken to the manse, the Methodist equivalent of a vicarage, which was to be our new home. It was a small four-bedroomed bungalow in the centre of a cul-de-sac and was surrounded by

21

conifers – from not one window could we see beyond them. It seemed hemmed in compared to the spaciousness of America, the tiny garden a postage stamp of grass for our lively children.

On the first night we arrived we put the children to bed and then sat in the living room of our new home without even unpacking our bags. Exhausted, Tessa was feeling overwhelmed with being in such a strange place with our young family. Suddenly we both felt very unsettled, and at two in the morning Tessa and I looked at each other and said, 'Let's not unpack our bags. Let's return to the States tomorrow. We'll apologise for wasting the time of the Methodist Church and say we've made a mistake.'

It was terrible, absolutely terrible – we were convinced that we had done the wrong thing even though there was no apparent reason, apart from our tiredness, for us to feel so discouraged. We had wanted to come, all the arrangements had gone smoothly without a hitch and we'd received such a warm welcome, so why were we suddenly feeling like this?

We've never experienced anything like it, before or since. We decided to pray and ask the Lord for help. We kept praying and praying and then at some point during the night the Lord revealed to both of us, almost simultaneously, that this was just a plain spiritual attack. We suddenly knew that the Lord wanted us here; that He wanted to use us for His glory and for the good of others. We asked the Lord to protect us from the enemy and we prayed, 'Lord, if this is truly You send us someone tomorrow to encourage us.' Eventually we got to bed, for a short night's sleep before the little ones woke up.

The next morning we got a phone call from Christopher and Linda Delbridge, a farming couple who attended Menheniot chapel in my section of the circuit. They were about our age, and they told us that they'd been praying for us, and invited us over for lunch. That just blessed us so much. That same morning Winney Ackerman phoned and talked to Tessa too. She was an enthusiastic Christian brimming with the Lord. She, too, said she had been praying for us and just knew the Lord had great plans for us here. God wanted us to know for sure He had answered our prayers!

The Delbridges picked us up and took us to their farmhouse. In conversation over lunch we knew we were among God's praying people and there was no doubt that God had prepared the way for us. We felt absolutely sure we were in the right place.

•∞•

We settled quickly into our new life; I suppose it helped a lot that we really loved England and the English people. Mind you, we didn't have idyllic thoughts about working here; we weren't looking through rose-tinted glasses, as you say! I think we realised how hard circuit work was going to be.

My main duties were centred around my assigned eight chapels, with my circuit superintendent residing in Liskeard, a town of around 8,000 inhabitants, about eight miles inland from Looe. At this point it may help to expand on how the Methodist Church works. In the early days of Methodism John Wesley had circuit-riding preachers whose whole life was spent going from chapel to chapel preaching to different congregations. In this way the early Methodists provided pastoral coverage for the numerous 'societies' that had sprung up during the Methodist revival in the 18th century. The structure continues to this day: a rota is usually drawn up quarterly in which the ministers are planned around the different chapels, and so you might visit some of your congregations maybe once a month. A minister can have anything from two to eight chapels in his circuit. There are exceptions if you are based at a large central hall, otherwise that's how every circuit minister works.

This system is quite a challenge, especially trying to get to know the people when you see so many of them for such a short time. Sometimes it's difficult to get to know them in depth and I found that one of the hardest things to cope with. There is also the problem of inconsistent ministry. The various preachers may have different theologies, and topics would change with the ministry each week. There was no possibility of teaching a series or following one sermon with another on the same topic.

We served in the Looe circuit for seven years. I think I served faithfully, I certainly tried to, and I worked my socks off; many Sundays I preached five times. My desire was to be faithful to my charge to preach the Gospel. I wanted so much to faithfully serve God, first and foremost, in this country. I think I realised that my evangelicalism could cause problems at some stage in the future but I didn't consider for one minute that to work in Methodism would be incompatible with my desire to serve the Lord...

The main chapel was called 'Barbican'. The congregation numbered twelve when we started and they were ready and willing to make whatever changes we felt the Lord wanted us to. Shortly after arriving, Tessa and I and the children knocked on the doors nearest our home and introduced ourselves. I don't think people knew what to make of this friendly outgoing American family!

The first summer a mission team came from Cliff College, an evangelical Bible College in Derbyshire, and during that time one of the neighbours dramatically came to the Lord. Another local couple, who wanted their baby baptised, also were converted. After that the numbers gradually grew but still there were plenty of people who never came near a church so I went out to meet them where they were. I regularly walked the streets all over Looe meeting people, asking them about their lives and sharing the Gospel in every way I could. I even went out on the fishing boats with the fishermen to find out what life was really like for them. I was terribly seasick; the first time I went out I ate two pasties at 4am for breakfast... the rest I leave to your imagination.

Shortly after we arrived, I spoke at an assembly in the comprehensive school down the road; I invited everyone to our house after school for doughnuts. That was the beginning of our weekly youth meetings! We have always loved young people and so we really felt for the youngsters of Looe. It made us sad to see that the kids had nothing better to do than to meet on the cliffs and blow their minds with alcohol and drugs. We had weekly Friday evening prayer meetings in our home. One week, after praying for the teenagers we decided we would go out to these kids and take homemade pizzas or cookies or sandwiches to share with them. In time we got to know them and told them about our love for Christ. They began to ask us questions and open up to us. We showed love and acceptance to them, even when they were aggressive and threatening. One of the young guys came to the church, accepted Christ into his life, and subsequently went to Bible College and is serving the Lord to this day.

At one point we hired the school gymnasium at Looe on a Friday night and invited young people in to play football and badminton. It was amazing; we would get eighty or ninety coming to play sport, and it was a great way of meeting kids and giving them something to do with their time. We also had a youth club at the Barbican building for a while and at another point, a children's club in the St. Martin's hall. A team of committed saints were beginning to get a heart for the needs around us...

We worked long hours but we were very happy. We were blessed during those years with the birth of our fourth child, Josiah, and our fifth, Katherine.

In the midst of our vigorous ministry we could not help but notice storm clouds brewing on the horizon. The Methodist Church at Conference (that is, national) level was beginning to deal with issues that would strike right at the heart of their historic commitment and my lifelong commitment to the authority of scripture and thus to the integrity of the Christian faith. We could never have imagined how our lives were about to turn upside down.

4

Trouble Brewing

I never set out to contest Methodism. I felt that I was a faithful Wesleyan Methodist. I believed passionately in the church's doctrinal standards, and I was committed to the vision of John Wesley; to preach a passionate Gospel, to see the world as his parish, and to offer Christ. I believe I was wholeheartedly committed to that… and happily so.

Throughout my Christian life I have been convinced that the Bible is God's Word, that ideas have consequences and that the stakes are immeasurably high. I believe God is precise and I believe that theology should be precise. We expect precision everywhere else; we don't want an airline pilot who's not precise, or a car mechanic who's not precise, or a surgeon who's not precise. But we are happy to put up with theologians who are imprecise, who interpret scripture to suit the time we're in, and that doesn't make sense to me. I believe the Bible is the revealed Word of God and that God presents the case in the Bible for His Son, and for our need of His Son, and I have a satisfied mind about those things.

I'm telling you all this to try to explain how I felt, and why I reacted the way I did, as events unfolded which tore my life, and the life of my congregations, apart…

• ∞ •

Every year I was required to attend Synod, which is the annual meeting of the local circuit ministers and their leaders. There I was expected to state that I agreed with the doctrines of the Methodist Church. Every year I had done this without hesitation.

But in 1993 the Church passed resolutions, one of which included the phrase: 'We recognise, affirm and celebrate the participation and ministry of gays and lesbians in the church,' and I knew that I couldn't agree with what was written.

I had seen this coming for a while… I'd almost made a stand and said no to the impending proposal the year before when I saw the resolutions coming. I almost thought this is ridiculous, but I didn't. Along with many other evangelicals in Methodism we hoped against hope that the Church would not allow itself to pass the resolutions at the 1993 Conference.

I believe the Conference was contesting its own constitution, by challenging the authority of the Bible, and that therefore the Conference had previously defaulted on its own constitution in 1992 when the Methodist Church affirmed in its own report that 'the weight of scripture was to teach that homosexual practice was incompatible with Christian teaching'. Yet the next sentence brazenly said, 'Nevertheless we do not yet have the mind of God on the matter', which betrays their opinion of scripture.

So if you're believing on the one hand that the Bible teaches something but that doesn't necessarily mean that you have the mind of God on the matter then clearly it betrays a low view of scripture, one incompatible with the historical position of Methodism on the Bible.[1]

---

[1] *I would like to emphasise here that the real issue at stake was that of the inspiration and authority of the scriptures, and the Methodist Church's departure from its own historic position stated in Wesley's 44 Sermons and his Explanatory Notes on the New Testament, which together originally formed the doctrinal basis for the Methodist Church. This departure was evidenced in the homosexuality issue, and to that extent it (the homosexuality issue) needed to be a part of this book. But the evidence must not be confused with the substance. There was one other area where it was evidenced in the 1993 Synod: that Synod 'congratulated' the World Congress of Faiths, which is a syncretistic religious think tank, the applauding of which by definition compromised the uniqueness of Jesus Christ. In the midst of the uproar over the homosexuality issue, this perhaps deeper and more tragic departure went unnoticed.*

My first allegiance is to the Lord. And the fact that I felt it was time for me to speak up is not a judgement on the many Methodist ministers who love the Lord. They have to do what they have to do and I honour those men because they have to live with their consciences. But I had to live with mine even though it meant that, if I was not prepared to agree to the resolutions, I may have to leave the Church I loved.

After the Conference when the 1993 resolutions were passed there was a flurry of activity among evangelicals in Methodism, all of us trying to figure out what in the world to do. A conference was held in Nottingham to discuss the issues, there were all sorts of letters flying around, and I was naïve enough and dreamy enough to believe maybe there would be an actual movement of evangelicals within the Church who would say, 'We're not going down this road, we're standing together; if you kick one of us out you're going to have to kick all of us out.' Yes, I was actually naïve enough to believe that maybe my little tiny effort would generate something and we could have righted the ship theologically.

The Synod was held in January 1994, in the little town of Porthleven, in west Cornwall. The night before it I was just scared to death; I thought there was no way I could go through with this. I was scared of having to go down there and take a stand. Because I felt that the Methodist Church had broken faith with their own constitution and with the scriptures I knew I had no alternative, but I would rather have died that night than go to the meeting the next day and take that stand.

I realised that it would have serious implications for me and for my congregations. I knew the chapels I pastored would stand by me, and I knew the Lord was with me, but I didn't like doing it. I was desperate, and the night before I was to go, the Lord gave me a scripture....

'Do not be afraid or discouraged because of this vast army, for the battle is not yours, but God's. Tomorrow march down against them. You will not have to fight this battle. Take up your position, stand firm and see the deliverance the Lord will give you. Do not be afraid, do not be discouraged, go and face them tomorrow and the Lord will be with you.' *2 Chronicles 20:15*

It really seemed that the Lord was trying to comfort and guide me.

The next day at the Synod I was asked, 'Do you submit to the discipline and doctrines of the Methodist Church?' I said no. I had to say no.

Knowing where I had come from and how much I wanted to serve God within this Church, it was unbelievable that I could be taking a stand against it. I could hardly take in what was happening, because I knew this would lead to the end of my dream to spend my whole life serving God as a Methodist minister.

I could imagine no other future.

5

Nowhere To Go But On

I t was a terrible, terrible period of my life, for me, my family and all those good faithful Methodist folk in the circuit who couldn't understand what I was doing. The fact that I had said no at Synod would not be the end of it – I would have to go before a church board in Exeter, almost as if standing trial, to decide my future.

News travels fast and the media began to take an interest, which compounded the stress. They were around all the time; reporters with cameras seemed to appear whenever we left the house. They'd picked up on the story and, sadly, homed in on the homosexuality issue, and suddenly I was news; my picture was in the local papers, on local television and it even reached the national press. I hate publicity and found it very painful. I was also sad that the press were focusing on the homosexuality issue. I would have made the same stand whatever, if I believed it went against scripture – it was never a particular issue with homosexuality – but there's no doubt in my mind that the media would not have been interested if I had been contesting almost any other part of the Word of God.

Some of the articles that appeared in the press were just not true. There were rumours flying around that I was deliberately trying to break away, aiming to build my own church, when it just wasn't what I wanted to do at all. I felt like I was being loyal to Methodism by standing up for the Bible, yet I found myself facing separation from the Church I loved and at the same time being vilified in the press.

It was like a death; no, worse than a death, it was more like a divorce.

However, God was close beside me and He graciously provided a companion for me for just a few days during that initial difficult time of media interest. Shortly before the scheduled Synod, Steve Schertzinger, a pastor from my university days who had been a mentor to me, had phoned to say he was on his way to Russia and wanted to stop in England to visit us. Now Cornwall is not exactly on the direct route between those places but with God's leading he ended up here. Steve accompanied me as I drove to Porthleven and was just outside the assembly room with his ear to the door when I took my stand. Afterwards he took care of my family, who were obviously very upset for me, and dealt with the media. That guy had never been here before, then he left and I haven't seen him since but he was definitely sent by God for that short time. It was a personal comfort from the Father to me.

I had been a Methodist pastor for thirteen years at that point and a Methodist all my life. I really loved that Church. One of the dreams I had was that I should be a force for good in the Methodist Church and that the Methodist Church should be a force for good for the Gospel for the world. I thought I might have a part to play in that. So I actually believed I was taking this stand out of faithfulness to Methodism and loyalty to my ordination vows. I actually believed that. Yet I was accused of being unfaithful to Methodism. And it was hard to be misunderstood by some.

There were many faithful and loyal Methodists who were caught in the pain of my decision through no fault of their own. Some chose to stand with me; some for whatever reason felt they couldn't. Nevertheless they too experienced the pain of the upcoming separation.

So it truly was like the end of a lifetime. I felt like my nervous system had been torn apart. My doctor gave me medication for depression and I have only come off it recently.

But that's enough about me for a moment. I was more concerned about my flock, as so many of them were supporting me, and I didn't

31

want them to be harmed by what was going on. I feared there would be a church split which would be painful for everyone. I discussed it with my assistant pastor, Martin Bunkum, who had supported me steadfastly throughout. On the Sunday following the Synod, I said to the folk at the Barbican chapel, 'I'm your pastor but if you don't want me to be your pastor any more I'll leave...'

Because I had made the stand I couldn't continue to pastor them in Methodism, so I had to tell them the brutal fact that if I was not allowed to remain as a Methodist minister, and if they still wanted me as their pastor, they would have to follow me when their Church removed me. And it wouldn't be easy for them. I repeated the message at the other chapels I pastored.

If they had said to me, 'Thanks for the seven years John, we think you're a great guy but we think you're completely wrong now, the Lord bless you as you go,' I would have left quietly, there would have been no acrimony, no issue; I would have just been someone who said no at Synod and had to go. But it wasn't like that. The issue was that these folks said, 'We want you to be our pastor, so we're behind you.' In a way it was wonderful to have that support, but on the other hand that's what caused the pain. They said, 'We are behind you, so when you go to Exeter know that we are praying for you, and whatever happens we will be with you.'

The trial in Exeter was set for April 19th 1994, so there was this terrible waiting time from the Synod meeting in January to April and that period was real turmoil. The press stayed around, constantly ravenous for news. I didn't enjoy their presence but I tried always to be patient with them. It was such a difficult time for Tessa too but as usual she was an unshakable support to me.

I was on the phone non-stop with the Evangelical Methodists around the country... there was pressure being put on me by church men in high places to just leave quietly and to just shut up, and I said, 'I can't, I believe I'm doing what's right.'

At one stage I even went back to the States to see my Bishop. He hauled me into his office in Arkansas and said, 'John, you're an embarrassment,' and demanded my immediate return to the USA. I replied that I was pastoring a group of people and it would be unfaithful for me to leave them.

The reason the Bishop had demanded my return was because the same rules didn't apply in the Methodist Church in the States, so I could have snuck back over there and remained a Methodist minister. I could have, but I had pastored people here who had told me they wanted me to be their pastor and I still felt called to minister in England. Oh, what a terrible choice!

In effect the Methodist Church was saying, 'You've been an embarrassment, you've made a mess of things, now get back here right now.' And I said no. They then said, 'OK, so you have two choices. Either face a church trial here, in America, or submit your ordination certificate and we will discharge you honourably.'

I felt like dying but I had to make a choice. I chose the latter option. In fact, what they finally did was they offered me something in the American Church once I was on trial here and thrown out. They offered me an honourable transfer which in effect then enabled me to pastor another church outside of Methodism. They transferred me out of their Church without any dishonour. In other words, they didn't want a fight. They could have defrocked me, they could have stripped me of my ordination, but they didn't and I'm so grateful for that.

I tried not to get bitter but I wasn't perfect by a long shot. There were times when I should have kept my mouth shut, when I got angry at people. That scripture I read from the second book of Chronicles, where it says, 'You will not have to fight this battle. Take up your position, stand firm and see the deliverance the Lord will give you,' really spoke to me and I tried to learn to just keep my mouth shut and let procedures happen.

There's a procedure in the Bible for dissenting, because you have to honour the authorities over you. You see it in the book of Daniel, when he was told in effect, 'Daniel, you are no longer allowed to pray to any God of your choice, and if you do you get thrown into the lion's den.' What Daniel did was he prayed to the God of his choice and then allowed himself to face the governmental consequences. And you see it in the Acts of the Apostles, where they said, 'Well you can beat us if you want to beat us but we can't stop talking about Jesus. So, we accept your authority to beat us but we're not going to stop; we're not going to have our consciences bound.'

Basically what I felt I did was this: I said, 'I have to obey my conscience and the Bible but you as a Church will have to do with me what you want to do. You do with me what you say.' And what they said was, 'We'll put you on trial and we will remove you.' I didn't feel there was a choice.

My family, my closest friends and the folks that I'd pastored talked the whole thing out. We knew it was going to cost spiritually, emotionally and financially. We'd just built a £70,000 extension on Barbican Chapel the year before because we needed the space, so we'd invested a lot into that place.

In spite of all the turmoil going on I felt that I had peace, though without joy. Whichever way I looked at it I felt that my position was right, I felt that I had done what was obvious to me, but it was a very sad time. There was so much loss.

One of the things that I've always been convinced of, but much more so even now, is that God rules His church by the Holy Spirit through the scriptures. It seems my life is a constant battle for the centrality of the Bible in Christian experience. I think in Methodism the battle was for the authority of the Bible. I think now the battle is for the sufficiency of the Bible. Is it actually enough? I believe it is. If a person feeds on God's Word, and if a church centres itself on the scriptures, will it be thoroughly equipped for life and Godliness?

I believe it will be.

•∞•

I don't want to go into the details of the trial, it's all behind me now. But to sum it up, on that day in April, in Exeter, they discharged me from the Methodist Church. It was awful. It was painful for the whole circuit, very painful, because it meant there was a huge public church split. It was painful for me because I was all of a sudden the focal point of a split. It was painful for the people who stood with me because some of them had to choose to leave Methodism, the Church they loved, believed in and hoped for, prayed for, longed for. Several were longstanding lay preachers; one had preached for nearly seventy years. Many were key members of one of my chapels, but in other parts of the circuit people were having their eyes opened to what was happening in the Methodist Church and were also distressed over it. The whole circuit was in an upheaval, the people I pastored were shattered. There was so much pain…

I was given around ten weeks to leave. We met for a prayer meeting one Saturday morning in Barbican, about a hundred of us, all stunned as to what we should do. We couldn't go back; there was nowhere to go back to. We'd burned our bridges and that was that. At the point when many of us felt like giving up we just knew we had to go on.

A gentleman in his 80's stood up and said, 'We've got to be like the children of Israel when they reached the Red Sea and Moses held up his hand and said, "Go on." We've got to go on.' And I think that all of us at that prayer meeting went home feeling we were like the tribe of Israel.

PART TWO

CHURCH ON THE MOVE

Brian Mitchell lives in Oxfordshire where he is an elder in an independent church fellowship.

In 1995 God gave him a unique role to play in the planting of Grace Community Church.

Brian tells his story...

6

'Does Your Husband Play Golf?'

My wife Yvonne used to attend the local chapel in Trewidland, near Liskeard, but the only time you would see me there was for special occasions, Easter, Christmas, christenings, that sort of thing… I couldn't see any reason why any person would want to attend a church. To be perfectly honest, I just couldn't see anything in this religion business whatsoever. I used to go just to keep the peace at home!

I was pretty sceptical in those days; apart from my wife I never really found anybody within the church who really actually lived what they said. Until I met John Gillespie.

I first met him just after he came to the UK; strangely enough, we got together by playing golf. I used to play (not very well), and John came to our house once to see Yvonne, spotted my golf clubs inside the door and said to Yvonne, 'Does your husband play golf?' That seemingly casual question became the beginning of a new direction in my life, though I had no idea at the time where it was to lead me.

So John and I played golf together and over a period of time I got to know him. I grew to respect his views because he lived what he said. He was very uncompromising. On the golf course we talked about all sorts of things and I found out that he had started a group for men in his home, which at that time was next door to the Barbican chapel in Looe. It was for people who wanted to dispute the Bible.

Well, that certainly appealed to me as I had plenty of things I could say on that subject!

I went along and watched as my objections were gently knocked down, one by one. I'd ask things like, 'Why do some people suffer? Surely if God is a God of love he wouldn't send anyone to hell,' and 'Isn't faith in one religion the same as all the others?' I had no idea that it was anything other than a discussion group, but of course people were praying for me, and the Holy Spirit was at work...

Then one night, after I'd been going to the group for about four months, I was at home and a strange thing happened. I had been reading James Bronowski's book, 'The Ascent of Man,' and I got to a particular chapter (in fact the bookmark is still in that chapter to this day) and I closed the book, and what happened next was nothing to do with that book at all, but for some reason suddenly I just knew that Jesus was my personal Saviour.

• ∞ •

The more I got to know John, the more I realised that he was different, and not only because he spoke with an American accent – within the Methodist circuit you get so many people coming from all different parts of the country as ministers that you get used to various accents, personalities, styles of preaching.... no, John was different because he was an evangelical who had no qualms about speaking his mind.

That was unusual within the Methodist Church.

Not only was John evangelical, he was also very enthusiastic and incredibly zealous. His energy was boundless. For instance, he set up prayer meetings at 6 o'clock on a Wednesday morning in a local chapel and a few of us would crawl out of our beds to meet there. But that wasn't all; he would have another prayer meeting somewhere else, as well as one for local preachers on Saturday morning at one of the circuit chapels. I went along on Saturday mornings because even though it was less than twelve months since my conversion I felt I had a calling to preach. Those meetings were wonderful; the people who went were really godly people and I was so inspired by them.

My faith grew rapidly. The more I studied the Bible the more I began to see it as the true Word of God, yet I had lingering concerns about the fact that the Methodist organisation was very liberal. It seemed to me that there was a group of people who were evangelical who wanted the chapels to grow, and there were others, mostly older, who took a more liberal view of the Bible and who almost didn't seem to see the need for growth. It was very strange. Sometimes you felt that maintaining the building fabric appeared more important than witnessing for its own sake.

I found myself quite confused at times; on Monday evenings I went to a Bible study run by John Hollins (a retired Anglican vicar who was a member at Barbican chapel), a wonderful godly man who was an out and out conservative evangelical, then on Thursdays I had joined a local preacher's course which was run by an out and out liberal who was very academic! It resulted in some very interesting discussions as I tried to marry the two viewpoints, which of course was impossible. I used to write essays as part of the local preacher's course, and received mixed marks because of my viewpoint. I had some fascinating conversations with the minister leading the course about how on earth the liberals expected to attract people into the Church as they were not offering anything the world didn't already give them.

During this time I was still trying to get to grips with the Bible, so although I was quite confused I didn't find it too disconcerting; I just kept listening to the different viewpoints and trying to weigh them up.

I took on a certain amount of responsibility within the church, initially as chapel steward and subsequently as circuit steward, so what with my full time job as a senior manager in industry... well, I was pretty busy.

Over the next couple of years, as I grew as a Christian within the local Methodist Church, I noticed that things were changing on the national scene and eventually the situation arose over John's stance supporting the authority of scripture at the Methodist national conference and we could see that things were going pear-shaped. I realised that at some point I was going to have to resign because I believed John's stance was honouring God and was determined to stand with him if it came to the worst and he had to leave the Methodist Church.

Although I knew I'd been called to preach I didn't feel at this point that it was honouring to God to be preaching in the circuit. I felt that the situation regarding John's stance was so awful that I couldn't stand up in a pulpit and preach the word of God with so much going on in the background, so I resigned as a local preacher in training and that didn't go down well. I stayed on as a circuit steward, but that didn't go down too well either because it was felt that if I couldn't do the one then I shouldn't really do the other, which is I suppose a reasonable point. Eventually the whole thing split apart. There were letters 'to the editor' in the press written vociferously against John, most of them anonymous.

It was tough but it was time for me to do what I thought was right; at a meeting in Liskeard I resigned as circuit steward, explained my reasoning and then the Methodist Church and I just parted. It was a surprising outcome for someone who had only been a Christian for five years, but I trusted God for what was happening and was determined to follow His leading wherever it took me.

7

Wanted, A New Home

After the split many members of John's congregations wanted to follow him. It was important that they were looked after, so we formed a small group of people to deal with the practical issues. I was asked to become treasurer of what would be the new fellowship (my wife said, 'How can you be treasurer – you don't even do the bank account at home?!' but for some reason I took the job on). We decided on a name for our new group. Some wanted the place-name Looe in the title; others didn't like that idea. In the end we decided on Grace Community Church. After all, God's grace had carried us through and, we believed, would continue to do so.

Most importantly, we needed somewhere to worship. By now we were a congregation of over one hundred, so it wasn't going to be easy to find premises to fit us all in, especially as we had numerous children in tow, all of whom were used to attending a lively Sunday School. There was no time to waste. We prayed and came up with the idea of using the local comprehensive school at Looe. We contacted them and they said we could rent their hall on Sundays, as they were under local authority pressure to earn as much as possible from their buildings.

It all happened so quickly; suddenly we found ourselves arranging the first service of the new fellowship in this new place. Almost overnight, with the wise advice of a few men who had become an informal leadership group, some of whom had great knowledge of churches, church structure and constitutions, we had become an evangelical church.

God was moving us on at quite a pace! There were many practical issues to attend to, so people took on various tasks. We stored hymn books in boxes under the stage at the school and one of our fellowship organised the purchase of Bibles so that everyone who came through the door would have a Bible to read. Various people brought instruments including a keyboard, full drum kit and guitars.

We didn't publicise the first service widely; we just told people in the area where and when we were going to meet. A group of us went ahead early the next Sunday morning and put chairs out without the faintest idea how many people would turn up. Many of us, particularly John, were still feeling shell-shocked.

We knew that the Methodists planned to have their normal meeting at Barbican chapel that Sunday morning and we felt uncomfortable; if a suitable place to worship had been available a few miles away we would have taken that, but unfortunately the school is only five hundred yards away from the chapel we had just left. We weren't intending to be provocative and were praying that it wouldn't seem that way.

To our amazement around two hundred and fifty people turned up at the school hall on that first Sunday. People came from Plymouth, twenty miles away, and even from other parts of the country because they'd heard via the media what John had done and wanted to offer their support. It was amazing, a real answer to prayer at a very difficult time. I recall that the service was very, very moving, but what I remember most of all was that the car park was full, and it was a big car park!

Just seeing all those cars made such an impression on me. Having so many people turn up seemed like the verification of the move John had made and from that point on we just felt that the Lord's hand was on it, in spite of the pain of the split.

· ∽ ·

Once we had a place to worship we had to address the very important matter of money. Previously John's salary had been paid by the Methodist Church; now we had to find the money from somewhere else. The members of the congregation knew the financial predicament we were in, and they just gave and gave; their generosity was overwhelming. The result was that we had enough money to pay John and his assistant pastor Martin Bunkum, who had followed him from Barbican, and we were able to pay them the same rate that they were getting at the Methodist Church; all this out of our congregation's seemingly bottomless pockets.

We also undertook to pay the rental on the house where John and his family still lived. Previously this had been paid for by the members at Barbican chapel, so we arranged for the lease to be transferred to us. Thankfully, a year earlier when their sixth child was on the way, we found a house to rent that would give more room than the manse.

Barbican rented the manse to others and added a top up to lease the 'new' place for them, which had no ties to the Methodist Church. After the trial, by the time John was officially discharged from the church the family was already out of the manse and were able to stay settled where they had been living for over a year. God had this, too, in hand.

Over the following weeks I discovered in my new role as treasurer that there were plenty of loose ends to tie up. I had to negotiate with the Methodist Church because some of our music equipment had been bought privately by people at Barbican. Some of them were kind enough to let us keep the items they'd given, such as drums and a keyboard. Another person donated hymn books. In the end we had what we needed and we were able to continuing making music to the Lord!

• ∞ •

Gradually the media interest died down, the letters page in the local paper no longer mentioned John, and we were left to our own devices. Although John continued to suffer emotional pain and depression, he was able to teach and preach, supported very ably by Martin, and as things settled down we fell into the security of a pattern of worship and teaching in the school hall on Sunday mornings and evenings.

Our numbers grew steadily. The Looe area attracts large numbers of tourists, so during the summer months our fellowship was swollen with many visitors from various parts of the country. John and his family were thriving and everything seemed to be going well. We felt we had everything we needed and that God had provided so bountifully for us.

• ∞ •

One Saturday morning while John was out at a meeting Tessa opened a letter addressed to Grace Community Church to find that the school was giving us six weeks' notice to leave their premises. Originally they had given us a six-month contract and said they would review it again at that point, and although our six months had just passed we had not had any indication that they would want us to move, so it came as a complete surprise. This news was very disturbing, as we knew there were no other properties in the area big enough to accommodate our congregation and their cars.

It felt like a major blow! We were settled, we'd got used to meeting there, we had places to store our equipment... we were, in a word, comfortable. We'd been meeting in the school hall for months and now we had only a few weeks in which to find somewhere else. We'd intended to stay there for years! Where else could we go?

That very same morning Mike Critchley, a member of our church, was, unusually for him, scanning the property pages of the local newspaper. Bearing in mind that John and Tessa now had six children and that they were being educated at home – there would be a need eventually to find the family a larger home, preferably one with four or five bedrooms. Mike's attention was drawn to a house in a hamlet near Looe with a large number of bedrooms. He tore the advert out, rang Tessa who called in and collected it and subsequently showed it to John when he got home. That afternoon John rang Mike and, during their conversation, dropped in the comment: 'The house has a barn attached to the back of it. Do you think it could be turned into a church?' It seemed to be a throw away comment and Mike didn't take much notice.

I can't speak for the others but when news that we had to leave the school premises reached me my first reaction was one of 'Why, Lord?!' I know that I should have given thanks in all circumstances, as the Bible instructs us *1 Thess 5:18*, but my feelings got in the way, and all I could think was why should John and the rest of our congregation have to go through this so soon after everything else that had happened?

At first there was confusion and a smattering of panic but then we got down to praying about the situation. God was at work and it didn't take us long to decide to accept it as His will, even though it was puzzling. So many of us had felt that the Looe area was where John was called to; many felt that this was exactly where Grace Community Church should be. But there was no other building in the area big enough for us to hire, so maybe we had got it wrong…

We prayed on, and the big question was, 'Lord, where do we go next?'

8

A House Called Oak Trees

The house in the advert was called Oak Trees. I don't know how many times I'd driven past without spotting it from the car. It's a big modern house in the hamlet of Morval, sitting slightly back from the busy road that runs from Liskeard to Looe. I must have passed it the day we got together to pray about our church's next 'home'. The number of times I'd gone by without the slightest idea of the part the house would play in all our lives...

By now our church had grown to a regular congregation of around one hundred and fifty people, including children. There aren't many buildings you can squeeze that number of people into, so our search for somewhere to worship became desperate. Our congregation came from a fairly wide area – some people travelled as far as twenty miles – so it was important that the venue was central.

The Public Hall in nearby Liskeard seemed to offer a solution, although it was likely to be a short-term option; we could meet there only on Sunday mornings as the place had been booked by other people for the evenings. Not an ideal arrangement but so what, we would find somewhere else to meet in the evenings. Except that it also transpired that we couldn't actually meet every Sunday morning because some weeks the hall had prior bookings.

But by now we were determined not to be defeated, so we decided to investigate the village halls in the area and see if any was available to hire. One of the places we went to was Downderry, a pretty little village on the coast, and there we found the Working Mens' Institute was available on Sunday evenings. Hooray! Naturally, people in the village found out what was happening and that had a knock-on effect; for example, someone who eventually became an important member of our fellowship and did a lot of work on our future church building got involved because we met in his village. This happened quite often; God brought people into our fellowship as we travelled around from venue to venue.

Then we discovered that the Guildhall in Liskeard was available so we arranged to meet there when we weren't able to use the Public Hall. At least we were spending Sundays in the same area, albeit frequently in different venues! The question was always, 'Where will we be next week?'

We eventually moved all our belongings out of the school and divided them amongst the fellowship members who faithfully carted everything around week after week. We really did feel like the children of Israel. We knew that we had to keep on trusting God and that He had the outcome in His hands. People responded wonderfully; everyone took turns at helping out and I can't remember a time when we were missing any equipment for a meeting. (Oh, and as a bonus some of us noticeably lost weight humping boxes and instruments!)

However, it wouldn't be true to give the impression that we were a constantly smiley band of people beaming our way around the Liskeard area as we worshipped joyfully in this place and that.

Moving from a morning service in Liskeard to an evening one at Downderry did cause some confusion. Not everyone in the congregation was happy about being on the move; many people felt that we should stay in the Looe area, with its dearth of lively churches, whilst it seemed that we were heading for Liskeard where there was already a considerable number of churches. We're only talking about a few miles geographically, but these things mattered to some of the congregation. The only thing we could do was to keep praying about it and as we prayed everyone felt God was leading us even though we were never sure where!

Not only did we have to find ourselves another church building, but also we would soon have to resolve the problem of securing a home for John and his growing family – by now the children were aged between eleven and one, and their rented house near Looe was approaching the end of the tenancy agreement. The fact that Tessa was home schooling all the children made it particularly important that they had stability and didn't find themselves moving around in the wake of our congregation.

So at the same time that we were looking for a permanent place to meet and worship, we also started searching the estate agents for a suitable property for our pastor and his family, one with plenty of bedrooms and living space, plus somewhere for John to use as a study, where he could talk privately and quietly with people. It was quite a tall order, and short of finding a country house, guest house or small hotel it didn't seem likely that many places would fit the bill. There was certainly nothing to suit our requirements in the local estate agents' windows.

Except for Oak Trees, that is…

The property was still available and when we studied the details we realised that it could be ideal for John and his family; not only was it in a convenient situation between Liskeard and Looe but also it had six bedrooms plus a self-contained annexe.

We quickly called a leaders' meeting to pray about it and the more we prayed the more it seemed just right to pursue the purchase of the property. The agents were seeking offers in the region of £100,000. Mmm, we thought, it seemed extraordinarily good value...

The only problem was that we didn't have any spare money; as treasurer I was particularly aware of our lack of funds. The congregation were giving so generously and somehow there was always just enough to pay John's and Martin's salaries, and for the rental of John and Tessa's home plus the hire of the various halls. In addition, we were tithing 10% of our income to mission work. There was a little left over each week but certainly not enough to buy a large rural property! And even if we could buy a house, there was still the matter of finding somewhere that would serve as a permanent church building.

Still, we didn't let those issues hold us back. We reminded ourselves that God owns the cattle on a thousand hills *Psalm 50:10*, so with just enough to meet our commitments and nothing to spare in the bank we decided to pay a visit to the house in the advert. At this stage we didn't contact the estate agents; it was obvious from the advert that the property was in the hands of receivers so, knowing it was empty, a number of us went and peered through the windows like a clutch of trespassing schoolchildren. At that point it became obvious why the asking price was comparatively low. We were shocked to see what a dilapidated condition this comparatively new house was in. As far as it was possible to see through the grimy windows it looked as if the insides had been ripped out of the place, almost as if it had been ransacked. We wondered how it had managed to end up in such a state.

Without doubt it would need refitting and redecorating from scratch, so that would mean even more money was required. Maybe this wasn't the right place for us, after all. Before we went back to our cars we took a walk around the back of the house and that was when something amazing happened. Adjacent to the rear of the house was a very large concrete-built barn or industrial unit, a high building with a big heavy wooden door on its end wall; apparently it had been used for storing potatoes. Now, believe me, I'm not into visions, but I remember this next bit so clearly...

We walked up to that place and found that the door wasn't secure, in fact it was partially off its overhead runner, and after a bit of shoving and pushing we managed to get it to slide across.

I'm not sure what we were expecting to find – after all, we were just being nosy – but as the door slid back and our eyes were adjusting to the gloom I saw the building full of people, standing up with their arms raised and all facing towards the far end of the barn! I was just amazed because as I said I'm not given to that sort of thing, so I didn't say anything to the others; I just thought, was that from God or was it just my imagination?

We all stood there not saying much as there wasn't really anything to say. (Unbeknown to me, two others of our group had the same vision, yet everyone kept their mouths shut!) Only then did I notice that the place was full of junk. We stared at the stuff littering the vast space; a boat, a caravan, piles of milk crates, concrete blocks, pallets, motorbike spares, old paint cans and endless rubbish. After a few minutes we heaved the door shut again and walked away, each deep in their own thoughts.

My mind was in turmoil but it was as if the Lord said, 'I'm in charge,' and I just couldn't shake off the impression that, unlikely as it seemed, I'd just had a glimpse of our future church...

9

The Margarine Tub

We went away and prayed again, and slowly it began to dawn on us what God had led us to: a house big enough for John and his family, with a building big enough for a few hundred people to meet in… big enough for the current church fellowship and more… We had been so busy searching for two places – a home and a church building – that it hadn't occurred to us that we may find somewhere to combine the two.

Suddenly the ransacked house and barn full of junk seemed full of potential! We had no idea what work would be involved to make it our own, nor how much it would cost, nor where we would find the money, but we knew, we just knew, that this was the place for Grace Community Church.

On the 26th March John told the fellowship during the morning service that we had found a property that would seem suitable both as a church building and as a home for his family. He added that we needed to know whether the congregation would financially support the plan to purchase the property.

My wife Yvonne cut a slot in the lid of a margarine tub, put a pile of pieces of paper next to it at the back of the room, and John told everyone that the box would be there for just three weeks. We were to pray about the property and if we felt that we wanted to support the purchase we should write on a piece of paper, anonymously, an amount of money we were willing to give at a future date, and post it in the margarine tub as a pledge. This sum of money should be in addition to what we all normally gave, and specifically to support the possibility of buying the property. It was quite a request, but at the end of the three weeks we would know for certain whether it was right to make an offer on Oak Trees.

We held an all day prayer and fasting meeting, and within three Sundays our congregation had pledged £67,000. The pledges ranged from £5 to many thousands of pounds. It was an awesome response and of course we took it as an indication that God wanted us to buy the property.

We were now in a position to negotiate with the estate agents, but we discovered that it was not likely to be a straightforward sale. The previous owner had gone bankrupt following the failure of his business, which had been conducted from the barn; in an attempt to keep his business afloat he'd tried to raise money at different stages by mortgaging the property in sections, creating in effect three different mortgaged lots. It was currently owned by three different banks and building societies who had come together under the receivership package.

The estate agents and a firm of solicitors, both in Plymouth, were acting on behalf of the receivers. We discovered that the house had been advertised widely in an attempt to find someone who was prepared to exchange money for a renovation project so challenging. So, as we began negotiations with the selling agents, we found that there were several other interested parties including at least one property developer. Again, we prayed; we didn't want anyone else to have Oak Trees if it was the place God had found for us. (We had no idea what the other interested parties wanted to do with the property, but I suspect no-one else was planning to use it as a church!) We asked God either to open doors for us or to ensure we saw that they were going to be firmly closed against us. At the same time while we were gathered together we discussed how much we were willing to offer.

Although the agents had indicated that they were looking for offers around the £100,000 mark they added that it wasn't going to be a race on price alone; a quick completion was just as important. Oh, and incidentally we were not likely to get it for as little as £100,000 in any case! So we prayed some more and decided to go to £110,000. We were keen for some indication that our offer was sensible but the agents said that they were not in a position to tell us whether the offer was realistic, or competitive, enough.

We were informed that, following our offer, the first group to submit a 10% deposit and exchange contracts would get the property. In our negotiations with the estate agents who were acting for the receivers on the sale of the property we were informed that when the contracts were completed we had to submit a bank transfer for the 10% deposit, which meant that if we were right about the price of the property our deposit would amount to £11,000… and all we had was a bundle of slips of paper in a margarine tub.

We thought and prayed about this and saw God work it out in an amazing way. By this time I was under notice of redundancy, which meant that I was in a unique position within the church fellowship: I had been given three months 'garden leave' so I had all the time in the world to do whatever was required, to be the 'runner', and I still had use of the company car with a car telephone (these were the days before mobile phones).

So during the days that followed I found myself freely nipping in and out of the estate agent's office in Plymouth, negotiating with them, ringing my colleagues back in Liskeard, keeping them up to date with the situation as it unfolded. I felt like an on-the-spot reporter, and it was an unforgettably exciting experience.

Somehow I began to get the impression that even £110,000 was not going to be a good enough offer, although the agents still wouldn't commit themselves to that fact. We knew that other offers had been received but we didn't know for how much. So after consulting my colleagues we agreed to increase the offer to £120,000 and this was faxed through to the receivers' estate agents. They in turn informed us that three parties had all made the same offer, so the first one to exchange contracts would secure the property. Contracts were sent out to all parties and received on Thursday 13th April, the day before Good Friday.

The situation was rapidly becoming daunting. The costs had escalated and the timing seemed impracticable. Easter was just around the corner – a time when not only are churches and congregations busy celebrating or going on holiday, but also when banks and businesses of all kinds take an extended break. We were going to need all the help from God that we could get!

Mike Critchley and John nearly wore a hole in Mike's lounge carpet that Thursday afternoon pacing up and down as they tried to come up with a plan. Eventually in desperation they went to one of the banks in Liskeard to ask for a loan one hour before it closed for the long Bank Holiday weekend. Understandably, they were politely shown the door!

What a challenge… if we really were serious about buying this property, somehow we had to exchange contracts, find the £12,000 deposit and organise a bank draft (a cheque was unacceptable) at a time when it seemed technically impossible. But we tried not to panic; nothing is impossible for God, we kept reminding ourselves!

10

A Welshman And A Postman

At this point a Welshman called Mr Phelps became a very important player in the unfolding drama. In fact the part he played is such a fascinating example of God's intervention that I'll tell you about it in detail.

Some time previously Mike had received a phone call one evening, while holding a house group in his Liskeard home. It was his friend Steve, from church, suggesting Mike ring a 'builder friend' of his in South Wales 'who's experienced at bringing churches back to life.' Mike, who had plenty of other things on his mind, made a mental note to ring the number and went back to the group, saying nothing. At around 11pm that night he was about to get into bed when Steve rang again enquiring why Mike hadn't yet rung his builder friend, to which Mike replied that he didn't ring anyone at that time of the night! Steve insisted, and much against Mike's better judgement he rang the Welsh builder friend, a Mr Phelps, who turned out to be awaiting the call!

Mike says, 'After a busy day I wasn't too keen to have a lengthy business call at that time of the night,' but he discovered that Mr Phelps had obviously been briefed on the situation we faced and went on to explain his track record refurbishing redundant church buildings in his area. Mike assumed he was simply a builder looking for work but then Mr Phelps said, 'I'll stay up all night and pray about it.'

The next day they talked again and Mr Phelps said that he would drive to Cornwall on the following Monday and view the property we had our eye on. Mike agreed to that but still didn't give it much further thought and it didn't occur to him to mention it to the pastors or other leaders.

On the Saturday Mr Phelps rang to say that he had found out that the 'girls' in the care home where he lived had baked him a cake for his 80th birthday on Monday and perhaps he should delay for a few days. This was obviously no local builder just looking for work to keep his lads busy!

A few days later Mr Phelps' son drove his father down from South Wales and he met up with Mike, John and Tessa, who showed him the potato barn with all its junk strewn about the floor. Apparently he took a glance around and with tears streaming down his face said, 'This is the place Lord.' Then he turned to John and Tessa and said, 'It's yours,' and finally he told Tessa, 'This will be the best house you'll ever live in.' Then he left. It was all over in less than fifteen minutes. His son drove him round a few local villages and then they returned to Wales.

• ∞ •

All this had been forgotten in the excitement of the impending exchange of contracts but now I recalled Mr Phelps' interest so it seemed right to ring him and introduce myself. I explained our predicament. 'What are we going to do?' I asked and he said, 'Leave it with me, I can sort this out.' Such was my lack of faith I exclaimed, 'But it's Thursday today and tomorrow's Good Friday!' Mr Phelps had the dignity and maturity to reply quietly and calmly, 'My bank manager will give you a draft for £12,000 for Tuesday.' I could hardly believe my ears.

Things were beginning to fall into place. We had contacted a Christian solicitor in Exeter, a friend of one of our fellowship members' team, who said he would do the conveyancing for us plus all the other necessary legal work free of charge, and he would try to do it as quickly as he could. Suddenly, unbelievably, we found ourselves in possession of the documents on the day before Good Friday.

By Good Friday I was virtually on my own; most of the leadership team had either left or were leaving the area to go to Spring Harvest, the annual Christian holiday convention, or to Caister, near Yarmouth, for the Fellowship of Independent Evangelical Churches' Easter conference. John was still around and he took the Good Friday service, feeling like he was experiencing the 'death of a vision' as we remembered the death of Jesus Christ for our sins. There was a real mixture of emotions running that day; some felt a real heaviness and wondered if there was any way possible for this amazing property to become ours. Because I was right in the middle of the process I felt hopeful even though it seemed a crazy situation.

Yvonne and I should have been away too, but we hadn't booked because I had expected to be working at this time. But of course God had arranged for me to stay at home because I would be needed in the Liskeard area over the Easter period; His perfect timing!

All stops were pulled out: one of our members took the contract to Exeter on his way to Caister; the solicitor worked on it over the weekend, pulling favours on the people he knew in the Land Registry office and other necessary places and rang me on Saturday to say, 'I can complete this and get it back to you in the post and it will be there on Tuesday morning.'

On Easter Sunday, there was a real buzz in church. Most people in the congregation had heard about the property and everyone was being so kind and generous; after the service two people came up to me and offered to mortgage their homes if necessary, to raise whatever was needed to achieve the final amount of £120,000. They said that the Lord had laid it on their hearts.

The next challenge was how to get the contract to the solicitors in Plymouth as early as possible on the Tuesday morning, when it wasn't due to arrive with us by post until later that same day. Mike Raymont (a businessman in our church) and I put our heads together and between us we came up with an ingenious plan involving my wife's cousin who was a local postman.

On Sunday I rang the postman and asked how I could get my post delivered as early as possible on the Tuesday. When I explained he said, 'Well, funnily enough I'm on your round that day.' He added, 'I can't let you have the package beforehand because that's illegal, but if you intercept me on the round I'll give it to you as soon as we meet.'

Bank Holiday Monday passed by in a blur of excitement. I set my alarm for the crack of dawn on Tuesday morning, drove to the village where the round started, received the precious package containing the contract, took it home and read it from top to bottom. It had to be signed by somebody from the church. I prayed and thought, 'Oh no, it's got to be me, everyone else is away.' I was on my own and I certainly felt it! Suddenly I had a moment of panic and thought, 'Lord, what have I done?' but I kept praying and soon felt a sense of peace, and so with a flourish of my pen I committed myself and the church to spend £120,000, knowing there wasn't a penny in the bank other than the bank draft that may or may not be winging its way to our bank at that moment from a man I'd never met!

I drove the twenty miles to Plymouth, straight to the solicitors but because I'd intercepted the post so early their offices weren't even open. I sat in the car and prayed some more and watched for the office door to swing open a chink. At one minute past nine I handed in the contract, it was recorded as a timed document so that was that; there was nothing more I could do so I drove home and waited. To say that I was nervous wouldn't begin to describe the feeling in the pit of my stomach, in spite of all the prayer. Nervous, but excited too.

After what felt like an interminable length of time I had a phone call saying that our contract had been exchanged, at 9.30am. I later learnt that the next contract arrived at 10 o'clock, so one of the other interested parties had pulled out all the stops too, but it was just too late – that half hour had made all the difference in the world.

Still praying, I rang the bank to check the balance on our account and discovered that it was miraculously in credit to the sum of

£12,000. To this day I have no idea how Mr Phelps managed to organise a bank transfer over an Easter weekend.

It felt absolutely amazing. We'd exchanged contracts. Oak Trees was ours! Okay, we still had to turn the pledges into actual money but God's hand was so obviously on the whole endeavour that by now the money seemed almost a minor detail. I rang the others at Spring Harvest and Caister, sharing the miracle with them. We were buzzing with excitement. I don't think any of us could really believe that we were now the owners of a house for John and Tessa and that, finally, our church would have a home of its own!

11

Nothing Short Of A Miracle

I have never felt so moved as I was by the generous spirit of the people in our fellowship during that time; it was humbling to see their willingness to give so selflessly. The money just kept rolling in. In the initial stages people were handing money over without documentation; later we organised it properly for those who could only afford to lend rather than give. Most of the money came from within the fellowship, but there were one or two Christians closely associated with Grace Community Church who also wanted to give a gift or offer a loan. The largest cheque was a six-figure sum from a Cornish Christian businessman not even involved in our church. He gave it as a loan with no interest and no repayment terms with initially no legal documentation other than the church sending him a sincere acknowledgement letter. (Incidentally, the loan was completely repaid by 2007).

When everyone was back from the Easter break and we had all calmed down a bit we added up the pledges, cheques and loans to find that we had £176,000! No major appeals or begging letters – just a margarine tub and a lot of prayer! It was enough money to enable us to buy the property and to budget for the renovation of the house as well as to commence the conversion of the barn into a church building. It was nothing short of a miracle.

By the time all the money had come in and a sense of order had been established I was handling several bank accounts, transferring money here, there and everywhere. God was enabling me to fulfil my role as treasurer with more confidence than I could ever have engineered myself!

The leadership team took some time out to meet and pray and to mull over what had happened. I relayed again the story of exchanging contracts, going over the details such as intercepting the postman, details that had so obviously been engineered by God. It had been a whirlwind time, and from where I was standing some moments had been really scary, but everyone's prayers had made such a difference and we all agreed that a sense of God's peace had permeated throughout.

We reflected on how God had walked ahead of us and made the way clear. It was a situation where you just knew that the whole thing was well under control, yet it felt strange because humanly speaking it shouldn't have been so easy; in fact it should have been terrifying. But the pace at which things had moved was helpful in a way; things had happened so rapidly there wasn't much time to stop and panic. The Lord just pushed it along. The speed of events had also prevented our logic getting in the way; had we had time to consider what we were doing I think we may have hesitated or done something different.

Anyway, we agreed, it didn't matter now – we had the property and the money to turn it into places fit for living and worshipping! All we had to do now was the work, and that wouldn't be a problem – with God!

On Wednesday 19th April 1995 we collected the keys from the agents and a group of us with our wives took a good look around our newly acquired building. Internally, the house was a wreck of a place, a shambles; the previous owner had torn out all the fixtures and fittings in order to sell them in a desperate attempt to raise money. Even the bath, toilets, radiators and the light fittings had gone; nothing remained but the shell of a house. However, we were relieved to find that it was structurally sound and had a good roof. Yes, we were particularly relieved because in the excitement of securing the property we had not even thought about getting it surveyed!

There was obviously a lot of work ahead but the first thing we did was to pray inside our future church building, this former potato barn. Prayer was still the priority and so we instigated a pattern of early morning meetings, sitting on concrete blocks among the clutter.

Our first move was without doubt the creation of a suitable home for John's family. Only once our pastor was securely housed would we focus on turning the shell of a barn into a place of worship. We realised that we were facing quite a challenge; the house was in such a mess that at first we had no idea where to begin. The greatest, almost overwhelming, task was to restore the plumbing; every room had bare pipes where the radiators, baths, sinks and toilets had been ripped out. We agreed that once we could see water gushing from the taps and hear toilets flushing in the background we would know we were truly making progress!

Oak Trees is a very large property so the original plumbing must have resembled a maze; there were pipes everywhere, and it was obviously not a job we could tackle without expert help. We asked my wife's cousin, who is a plumber, to give us a quote for the work. He was too busy to take on the job but said he would come and give us an idea of what it would cost. His face was a picture when he saw the state of the place, and his words brought home the enormity of the task. He said, 'This is going to take forever. Because the pipes have been cut off you'll need to start from scratch. Worse than scratch. It's going to cost thousands.'

The next plumber we contacted for a quote also told us that it would cost several thousand pounds… we declined his offer politely. The third plumber, Terry, was recommended to us but when we told him over the phone where the property was he seemed reluctant to come; it turned out he'd done the original plumbing work and thought we might be complaining about it.

Once he realised how badly we needed help he overcame his reluctance and turned up at the house with all the original plans and calculations for the pipe-work of the building. Initially Terry walked around aghast at the damage, but after he recovered from the shock he got down to work and became a true Godsend – with the help of the plans he knew exactly where every pipe should go and what thermal capacity the radiators needed, saving many hours of his time and consequently saving us a great deal of money. How many plumbers hold on to plans and calculations once they've finished a job? It was yet another gift from God.

Terry helped us in so many other ways too, including changing the previously fitted gas central heating to oil and charging us only for the replacement of the fittings. We explained what the financial situation was and he said he would try to get trade terms for the fittings so he made hardly any mark up on them. It was a very kind gesture and later he even donated a piano for our use!

As the interior of the house was so damaged we decided to take advantage of the disarray and change the use of some of the rooms. There were more bathrooms than John and Tessa would need, even with their large clutch of children, so we turned one of those into a bedroom. We put in shower rooms on the ground floor and I found myself doing things I had never done before such as fixing doors, skirting boards and shower bases as well as building a concrete plinth for the oil tank.

Obviously the project needed to be a team effort; however, because most people were out at work during the day it wasn't initially a very big team so anyone who volunteered found themselves with a job! I became unofficial assistant to yet another Terry, a member of our church who had been a Post Office engineer, and who was able to reconnect telephones and help in a dozen other ways. I found myself standing next to him, being passed wires and being told to 'Put this here and that there,' which I did, dutifully!

Everybody who was available just got on with whatever work they could do, and hour by hour, day by day the house began to resemble a home.

There were so many people involved it's impossible to name them all here, but I remember that one retired couple called David and Geraldine spent many days decorating and cleaning. Also, Mike Raymont and his team were involved in many of the decisions and activities regarding the conversion.

We were attracting plenty of outside attention. Being in such a prominent position on the main road we received endless visitors, mainly local people who came to see how things were going. Some days we spent almost as much time showing people around as we did working! Not everyone was friendly; there was a rumour circulating that we were a cult and some people turned up to challenge us. We tried to answer their questions patiently and courteously, to reassure them that we were just normal human beings.

One morning I was working outside fixing the doorbell when a man with a Scottish accent appeared saying that he was on holiday in Cornwall. He'd heard about Grace Community Church and the Oak Trees renovation project, and he wanted to come and give a donation. We spent some time talking about the project and he said, 'My brother has also heard about it and has asked if he could give a donation.' 'That's convenient, I happen to be the treasurer!' I replied, and as he was writing the cheque I asked him where his brother lived. He said, 'Oh, he lives in Peru.' I was intrigued, and asked him if he had told his brother about our church. No, he said, it was the other way round. His brother had contacted him from Peru, where he had heard the story of Grace Community Church, and had asked him to call in when he was visiting Cornwall to give a donation. I was overawed to think that somebody in Peru could have heard about our church. It was a real boost, a feeling of God's reassurance to us.

•∞•

The weeks passed and everyone who was available just got on with the work. People sanded, scraped, painted, cleaned, sawed... our fellowship seemed to draw on endless hidden talent. Looking back on it now it amazes me what we had the confidence to do, with minimal help from professionals. We just got on with it, pooling our diverse knowledge and ability. One of our members had worked for the local Electricity Board as an electrician, and as the house didn't need rewiring he managed to do all the work required to enable the electrical fittings to be put back in. Soon we could flick switches and we had lights and power. Running water, flushing toilets and now electricity... this was real progress!

The kitchen had been ripped out by the previous owner and through the generosity of someone who knew about our situation we managed to get the vast amounts of cupboards and work surfaces required for that huge room, for less than trade price. God was the master builder; He just kept paving the way, every day, even organising it so that the weather was fantastic all the time. We could work outside or inside, carrying equipment in and out, without worrying about rain.

There was a small annexe attached to the house, which looked as if it may have been designed as a granny flat at some point; it had a kitchen that we decided to refit for use by the church. Our kitchen fitter, Les, a really kind man, went to the trouble of offering us a kitchen he'd taken out of a house in Plymouth, which was destined for the tip. It wasn't in brilliant condition but it was ideal for our needs, and all we had to do was to go with him to transport it. Another church member, Glyn, was able to refit it into the annexe, so the Lord's hand was even in the fitting out.

There were no carpets in the house; they'd all been removed and no doubt sold. We started to get quotes, and that was scary because it seemed we needed miles and miles of carpet! We tried lots of places in an attempt to find something affordable but hardwearing, bearing in mind the number of young people who'd be running around the house. Because the square footage was huge we ended up searching further afield than usual, travelling out of county to the larger warehouses. But eventually God led us back home to a company in Liskeard, right on our doorstep, who gave us a remarkable price and threw in the fitting and underfelt free.

As I was holding the purse strings I was very tight on the budgeting for every single item; I didn't let anyone go over what had been allocated. Although I'd not been a treasurer before, I had been a project manager in business for a long time and was used to making sure people kept to budgets. I was constantly fending off supposedly useful suggestions for spending money. Someone would say, 'We could add this thingy here,' or 'Let's put one of those wotsits there,' and I got into the habit of replying, 'Well, we could, but we don't want to! The Lord's given us this money and we'll keep it as straightforward as possible.' In the end, thanks partly to budgeting but mainly to people's generosity we did all the work needed in the house for £10,000. It was unbelievable, we could easily have spent that on carpets alone.

As the date crept closer for John and Tessa to move out of their rented home more and more people got involved to help with the decorating and the cleaning. We purchased gallons of paint and everywhere you looked there was someone wielding a paintbrush. Teams of ladies and children and teenagers turned up with buckets, cloths and every type of cleaning fluid imaginable and scrubbed the house from top to bottom. It seemed that every room in the house was bustling with people and in the kitchen a bottomless pot of tea was kept brewing.

On the 13th July 1995 John, Tessa and their children, Bethany, Johnny, Jachin, Josiah, Katherine and Rebecca, aged between thirteen and two, moved in. It had taken three months of selfless effort and teamwork, the money and pledges of countless generous people and the controlling hand of God to create a lovely new home for our pastor and his family.

· ∞ ·

So, that was the end of phase one. Now we had to turn our attention to establishing our church in this place God had prepared especially for us. All we had to do was to convert the barn.

Ah, but there was just one small problem – we hadn't actually got any planning permission…

12

Leaping Over Hurdles

At some point during the restoration of the house we'd decided to meet on Sunday evenings in what had once been the billiard room, so by the time the house renovation was completed we'd actually been worshipping on the site for a little while. It was perfectly adequate for the needs of our evening meetings, which attracted a smaller number of people than in the mornings, and we thus saved some money on the hiring of halls. These were informal meetings, not conforming to the usual concept of 'church'; they worked well but in order for us to establish Grace Community Church so that we could accommodate our full fellowship we really did need planning permission.

We knew when we exchanged contracts that Oak Trees had no planning permission whatsoever other than for normal residential use, but we had felt so strongly that it was the right place for us that we put aside the issue for the time being.

Now we set about praying and planning our next move. Our first line of approach was the parish councillors, who informed us that whoever had owned the place before had tried to get planning permission for business use, with no success. Permission was turned down for various reasons, including access because the property was on a main road. The parish council said they had no objections but even if they passed it they were sure we would get no further with the application at district council level, and certainly never get planning permission for a church. Oak Trees was a residential property and that's the way it would stay, we were informed.

By now we were used to leaping over hurdles and we knew for certain that God had other plans, so rather than being daunted by this news we kept on praying, believing that when the time was right God would sort out the matter of planning permission.

God went ahead of us yet again. By the time we had finished refurbishing the house a man called Graham Laywood had joined our fellowship and kindly offered to draw up the plans for the application for permission to convert the barn into a church building. We discovered that Graham was no less than Prince Charles' quantity surveyor in the Duchy of Cornwall!

We submitted an application for change of use from residential to church premises, and three of us attended the parish council meeting where the plans were heard. We were told we could sit in on the meeting up until the time when our application was going to be discussed and then we would have to leave, which is what we did. We waited outside, and prayed.

As we had been warned, they passed it on the understanding that the district council would refuse it; apparently the parish council couldn't refuse it anyway as it was outside their remit to pass or reject it. It seemed we were wasting time but we knew it was important to follow the correct procedure. The next stage was the district council meeting to be held in Liskeard, some weeks later. Again, all we could do was wait and pray.

Whilst the parish council had been approachable and amenable, there were people on the district council who didn't want us to succeed, mainly because of the publicity that had been raised when John left the Methodist Church. The rumour was still circulating that we were a cult requiring our 'members' to pay £10 or £20 each week into funds just to attend Sunday morning meetings, and that didn't help matters. Fortunately God had ensured that there were also people on the district council who did want us to succeed, one of them a gentle Christian man who spoke eloquently at the meeting in support of what we were trying to do.

We half expected to be turned down at the first application and had prepared ourselves for umpteen different submissions. We needn't have worried; our application went through at the first attempt in contradiction to most of the advice we had received. We were absolutely delighted, and thanked God for His generosity to us.

Certain restrictions were imposed on us, in particular concerning the number of cars we could park outside the building, but we didn't let those worry us, and in any case they were all eventually rescinded.

• ∞ •

Although I didn't know it, my time with Grace Community Church was coming to an end, and just after planning permission was obtained God organised for me to bow out. One of the job applications I had made several months earlier turned into the offer of a well-paid position in Abingdon, near Oxford. The job offer was received the day John and his family moved into Oak Trees; how about that for amazing timing! My garden leave ended, the car and its phone, both of which had seen extensive use during the building phase, went back to my previous employers and my wife Yvonne and I began to plan our next move.

In one sense I was sad to be leaving just as the church was beginning to be established in a permanent building – I would love to have worshipped there, at least for a while, but on the other hand I was looking forward to the next phase of my life knowing that God was in control. As I prepared to move away I looked back on the events of the last couple of years and many thoughts went through my mind.

Our church had been virtually in exile, had gone through such difficult and challenging times, and John had suffered more anguish than we would ever know. But we had tried to stay faithful to God and had trusted and followed Him until He put us exactly where we were meant to be. Many of our congregation had felt initially that Morval was the wrong place for Grace Community Church to be established because it was in the countryside, seemingly in the middle of nowhere. But one member who saw it differently said: 'Look at it like an aircraft carrier. We have a base, but we go out from here,' which was an unusual but accurate way of putting it.

On a Sunday morning several months later the potato barn was packed to overflowing, as Grace Community Church celebrated joyfully the first morning service in its new home. Compared with the house renovation the work had been relatively straightforward; we had simply created a wooden framed building inside the barn itself. It would never, externally, be a place of beauty, but after all it is the people who are important, not the building!

By then Yvonne and I had moved to Abingdon but we returned for that first Sunday in the new building, and as we walked through the outer door into the main hallway I was amused to see dozens and dozens of shoes placed neatly by the door, and to see everyone filing in, young and old in their stockinged feet... The varnish on the floor was not quite set.

Nobody cared. Absolutely nothing was going to stop us from worshipping in our new church on this very special day. I'm sure God was smiling!

PART THREE

WARTS AND ALL

Mike Critchley has been with Grace Community Church from its inception.

He talks candidly about some of the things that have happened since then, things that make the church family what it is today...

13

Growth

' The youth are our future, our springboard,' said John at one of
the church's annual meetings, where our whole church family
gathers to review the past year and to set goals for the next.

Today Grace Community Church's emphasis is on mission and
training and creating a place where people come for as long as they
need to, whether for short or long periods. It's a base for youngsters,
where they are given the grounding to enable them to take the next
step in their walk with God, whether it be in the local community,
training for the ministry or missionary work in the four corners of the
world. Budding ministers are inspired to go on to Bible School and
supported wherever possible, financially and spiritually, by both our
church and other church leaders in the area. With the dedication and
encouragement of a team of experienced youth ministers the Grace
youth church has grown beyond everyone's expectations. Some of our
young people have parents at the church, others come along with
friends, but many simply come on their own.

Jesus' last command was, 'Go,' *Matt 28:19* and until He says,
'Don't go,' we will continue as a church to send people out. So many
missionaries have come out of Grace that sometimes it's a challenge
to keep up with their news, which arrives from all parts of the world,
including Peru, Portugal, India, Taiwan, Senegal, Hawaii, Papua New
Guinea, Kosovo and France. Although most of the missionaries have
come direct from Grace, some have been adopted by us as 'mission

interests', usually as a result of overwhelming interest in their work or organisation.

•∞•

When Grace Community Church began it was unusual within Cornwall because it drew people from a large area, and still does to a certain extent; our congregation are unlikely to bump into each other in the local supermarket during the week. The main basis of our church is the many house groups that meet over a wide area and who come together to worship on a Sunday morning. Each group is a small community in itself, where people can share problems and draw from the closeness that develops when folk are willing to be real about what is happening in their lives.

Although there are plenty of people at Grace who have been in the church since the very beginning there are always new faces to be seen; some are visitors on holiday, but others may stop with us for maybe just a year or two before God moves them on. The leadership believe that a flow of people through our church is healthy, as long as the main core membership remains constant. New people bring new ideas and maybe new leadership potential. Whatever the time of year, even in deepest winter with snow on the ground, the visitor's corner in the main meeting hall is never empty. Members of our fellowship are designated to spot newcomers and we always try to offer an attentive and warm personal welcome to everyone.

Over the years so many people have been drawn to Grace that eventually we had the joyous problem of overcrowding, as the church building began to split at the seams. The potato barn that had seemed so vast when we first peered inside began to feel the squeeze of a very large congregation; at one point there were regularly thirty or forty people standing at each service simply because there was nowhere for them to sit!

We must have been breaking many a health and safety regulation and we knew it couldn't continue.

Convinced that the only way forward was to double the size of the church premises we put in for planning permission to create a building alongside the current one, to enable the congregation to expand from 250 to 500. The church prayed. The application for planning permission was turned down. Ever optimistic, we submitted the proposal again; we appealed against the earlier decision and prayed some more. Again it was turned down, this time on grounds of sustainability. Eventually it became apparent that God had other plans. We reflected that maybe in our enthusiasm to expand we hadn't listened closely enough to God; to get to the point of being turned down twice had cost much in time, money and heartache.

At that point there were lots of people travelling fifteen miles from Torpoint, a town of around 10,000 people close to the Cornwall/Devon border. Suddenly it seemed logical to set up a church plant there. Once the idea was conceived Torpoint Community Church was born almost overnight. The local primary school made their hall available and with Martin Bunkum as pastor this new lively church quickly became part of the local community; every week sees a large number of non-Christians in the congregation and in the two Torpoint house groups. And the problem of overflow at Morval was alleviated.

Meanwhile, another new church was in the pipeline. One of the Grace house groups, based in the original county town of Bodmin, had grown to around twenty-five members and out of the group came a desire to establish a church. The local primary school hall was found to be available and a brilliant deal was struck; no money changes hands but we are asked to go into the school and take RE lessons – a win/win situation! Following an initial year of relying on member leadership and visiting preachers from Grace Community Church Richard and Alison Powell took over the pastorship. With the planting of the friendly and welcoming Bodmin Community Church the Grace family of churches had become three.

All our churches reach out naturally into the community: between them they cover a range of involvement in hospital visiting, helping staff at a pregnancy crisis centre and summer outreach evenings in Looe; there are ladies away days and outreach events for men; teams go into old people's homes and take services. The Grace ethos is, and always will be, one of servanthood. We encourage members to get fully involved in their local communities and the range of involvement is diverse, from the District Council to mother and toddler groups.

14

Ouch, It Hurts

Expansion and progress bring delight, but they bring growing pains too. Everyone knows there's no such thing as a perfect church and sometimes God allows tough things to occur to bring a church back down to earth.

Several years after its establishment Grace Community Church appeared to be going from strength to strength; I think at the time that we believed we were a successful church. However, unbeknown to the congregation trouble was brewing in the shape of one couple's marriage problems. What made it particularly difficult was that the husband concerned was Martin Bunkum, our salaried assistant pastor and one of the men who had stood by John from the very beginning. As a direct result of the pressure of his position within the church his marriage began to fall apart.

As Martin says, 'My role grew out of all proportion to the time I had to fulfil it and in due course I suppose I became married to the church.' He was trained to deal with marriage counselling yet ironically he was spending so much time on church work that there was virtually no time left for his wife Sharon and their three children. At the end of each day he was going home with nothing left to give.

The marriage floundered for months as the couple tried to conceal the fact that they had problems. Certainly no one at Grace appeared to have noticed, or perhaps people were simply ignoring the warning signs until, to everyone's amazement, Martin and Sharon separated and began divorce proceedings.

The church was rocked to its foundations. What was going on? Surely a church pastor can't be in this situation? Here we were, a flourishing, apparently successful fellowship, and we didn't know how to handle the fact that one of our pastors was having marriage problems. The situation rumbled on and on, everyone hoping that the Lord would sort it out and all would be resolved, given adequate time.

But it wasn't to be... heads remained firmly buried in the sand and the problem didn't go away. Something had to happen to resolve the issue. At that point I was the church secretary and had no choice but to get involved. I knew we needed expert advice, so I rang our umbrella organisation, the Fellowship of Independent Evangelical Churches (FIEC), to seek advice. It felt as if we were the only church this had ever happened to, but of course that was not so. A wise advisor at the FIEC reassured me that, sadly, this scenario is not uncommon in churches. He directed me to a specialist within their organisation, who proffered some very tough advice: 'You need to sack the person involved, as he should not be in leadership in these circumstances. It will be the best thing for him and for the church because then the healing can start.'

I decided that we needed to get proper legal advice, too, and reasoned that there must be a Christian solicitor somewhere who would empathise and advise. I started by ringing the Lawyers Christian Fellowship in London asking if they had a suitable specialist who could help me. By this time I was desperate and would have travelled anywhere in the country to get the advice needed. To my amazement I was told that their expert in this field was based in Plymouth, less than twenty miles away!

Once I had gathered all the information I needed, I met with the rest of the leadership to discuss our next move. It was a dreadful situation; Martin was my friend and I was about to propose that he be sacked. After much prayer and discussion we agreed that to ask Martin to leave was the only, and indeed the best, option. In due course that happened, and even though no doubt many people had been expecting it for weeks, it hit the church like a bombshell.

When I reflect on this very difficult period it seems to me that we were so busy thinking we had got it right that we failed to notice that the real world, the world of broken marriages and rejection, was right inside our church. It was the result of just one leader being over-worked and believing he should take on everything that was thrown at him. He had been put on a pedestal and it was our fault. It showed us that even pastors are fallible and it certainly revealed a gap in the way the church functioned. This was Grace Community Church, warts and all. We were embarrassed and we just didn't know how to cope.

By now Martin and Sharon were attempting to mend their marriage but had left the church, feeling rejected by our congregation.

For a while all went quiet while the matter was swept under the carpet. But eventually it was obvious, once again, that something had to be done to resolve the problem so two of the church elders went to the couple's home and the painful journey of repentance, forgiveness and reconciliation began. Martin was seething and told them exactly how he felt, that he and Sharon had experienced coldness and rejection from the church and that he'd been put on the scrap heap. He was not condoning his or Sharon's actions and was fully aware of their responsibility to put things right, but he said that when they had most needed help, the help had not been there. He was right.

The two elders did not try to defend themselves or the church; they received the criticism graciously, which set the right path for healing. It was decided that the way forward was for the couple to meet with all the elders to apologise for their extra-marital relationships, and then to attend a church meeting to apologise to the whole church for their behaviour.

It was terribly painful for everyone but afterwards the elders made a point of telling the congregation that the matter had been dealt with in the correct way, that the episode was in the past and as a church everyone was now going forward. Eventually Martin was reinstated as assistant pastor and, of course, in time became pastor of the new

Torpoint Community Church. It was an amazing exercise in forgiveness and restoration for all parties.

So, the issue had been correctly dealt with; however, it left so many questions unanswered. How could a Christian couple, especially a leader and his wife, get themselves into such a mess? How could an apparently successful church deal so badly with the situation? And why had it happened in the first place? It was a wake up call and as a church we needed desperately to learn from it. The church is basically (unfortunately) middle class and maybe, without our realising it, because of that came the pressure to be successful. Looking back, we had probably become arrogant and that was why we had such a long way to fall.

It was a very traumatic time but the lessons we learnt were crucial and God obviously allowed it to happen for our growth. We learnt to treat the pastors as human beings rather than commodities; to allow them more time for their families by sharing the load. We learnt that when issues like this arise they have to be faced head on – they don't go away of their own accord. The church has to make every effort to get advice from people who've been this way before, which in itself is a brave move because you're putting your hand up and admitting that something's going wrong, that in fact you're not the perfect church. We were reminded that churches employ frail human beings that we put on pedestals at our risk. Leaders are vulnerable and they have temptations, as we all do. We contributed to our own downfall by thinking it could never happen to us.

But in the end what matters is what God does with us within the mess that we create, and God brought us through. Today we are without doubt a stronger church because of what happened.

15

The View From Here

Grace Community Church, still in its old potato barn, stands on a hill with wonderful views of the surrounding countryside towards the sea. If you are fortunate enough to be here as the sun sets on a clear summer's evening the spectacle is breathtaking. We're just a few miles from the beautiful Cornish coast, and the county's many attractions are easily reached by car... and if this is beginning to sound like a holiday brochure it's because believe it or not God has arranged it so that you can come to Grace for a holiday!

Adjoining the church and its car park are two large fields. In 2002 we felt that God wanted us to use these fields to start a camping Bible Week, where people from all over the country could come for physical and spiritual refreshment. The church prayed. An opportunity arose to buy the seven-acre field just behind the church and also to use an adjacent three-acre field. It was obvious that God had provided just the right site so with His direction we began to plan Bible Week, the aim of which, as John says, is: 'To embrace whole-heartedly the opportunity to give, serve and bless the wider church in this country.'

Bible Week is a wonderful time set aside for fun, fellowship and teaching. The ministries are held in five marquees, one seating 600 adults and four smaller ones for the young people. Our church building transforms into a café, a place of relaxation and a handy refuge from the occasionally capricious Cornish weather. Accommodation is in tents and caravans, though some choose to stay in local guest houses or hotels or log cabins adjacent to the camp site.

Each year more than 150 of our church members from Grace, Torpoint and Bodmin Community Churches use their gifts in whatever way they can to ensure the smooth running of Bible Week. There's no shortage of jobs: cleaning the toilets and shower block; running the crèche; cooking and serving hot dogs; keeping a vigilant eye on the sound system; arranging the flowers that adorn the marquees; taking turns on night watchman duty... everyone pitches in to help. We've all discovered new gifts in the process; I've even found I can cook a mean beefburger...

Visitors come from throughout the country, and they keep coming come back for more. They return mainly for two reasons; they say very kindly that our church family serve them well but also they come for the teaching, which is shared by John and an invited preacher who varies from year to year, as well as leaders from within our church. John's teaching in particular is never compromising and it's not uncommon to hear the Biblical perspective of lust, divorce, same-sex relationships and a host of other potentially prickly topics expounded in the main marquee. Meanwhile in the children's marquees all age groups are catered for and this gives parents a welcome opportunity to take time out knowing the youngsters are ably looked after.

The ambience of Bible Week is one of a large extended family get-together: it's wonderful to see the children running around the fields shouting and laughing in such a safe environment. Between adults new friendships are quickly forged, especially when you are under canvas and sharing food and gear. Groups gather around barbecues and families welcome single people into their tents for meals. The joy and friendship rebounding around the campsite is tangible, and many of those who return year after year are now counted as dear friends by the congregation.

We pray for every camper for several months before they arrive. As the weather breaks each spring we begin holding prayer meetings outdoors, praying for all that will go on as we disperse to every corner of both fields. The work that goes into Bible Week is enormous but it is without doubt one of the highlights of our church year and has blessed us beyond measure.

And so life goes on in our family of churches in Cornwall, with our ups and downs, joy and pain… all against a backdrop of Bible teaching and study, prayer and repentance, learning lessons and turning again and again to God.

As this book ends there is yet another joyous problem of growth at Grace Community Church; we have an urgent need for more space for all our young people, from the crèche upwards. God is working it out, as usual. He conveniently planted an architect in the church at just the right moment; she drew up plans for an extension to accommodate the youth, an application for planning permission went to the District Council and this time it was approved unanimously!

One thing remains – there's the small matter of £250,000, which we need to complete the building work. It's a lot of money, but as a church family we're taking a fairly relaxed approach. As someone said, 'No problem, we've done it before, we'll do it again. We just need to get down on our knees. And while we're at it could someone dig out that old margarine tub…?'

Pastoral Letters...

*The following pages contain letters
written by John Gillespie to his church family.*

*We hope that you will find some
help and guidance in these.*

Praise be to the God and Father of our Lord Jesus
Christ, the Father of compassion and the God of all
comfort, who comforts us in all our troubles, so that
we can comfort those in any trouble with the comfort
we ourselves have received from God.
For just as the sufferings of Christ flow over into our
lives, so also through Christ our comfort overflows.

2 Cor. 1:3-5

Dear Brothers and Sisters,

I want to encourage us today with a powerful truth from the Word of God. It is a truth that has the power to transform situations where pain and suffering seem to be overwhelming.

The scripture passage above gives a value to suffering which transforms it from a lonely, forsaken road of anguish to a meaningful avenue of ministry. The passage tells us that suffering and pain ('troubles') actually have a redeeming quality to them, which delivers the sufferer from the double tragedy of suffering with futility to the redemptive tragedy of suffering with purpose.

Explore the passage with me, and I am sure that you will see this glorious truth as I and countless other followers of Jesus have.

Notice first of all that the Apostle Paul adopts an attitude of praise to God, the 'Father of Compassion, and the God of all comfort', not because God has prevented suffering from coming his way, but because He has 'comforted [him] in all [his] troubles'. The ancient Apostle does not have a rose-coloured view of life. He is realistic. Life can be tough, but God, our compassionate Father, comforts His children in the midst of the suffering.

But the sentence then delivers to us the truth which can be revolutionary for the one caught in the current of a troublesome time: '...[God] comforts us in all our troubles so that we can comfort those in any trouble with the comfort we ourselves have received from God.' Here then is the redemptive power of suffering which delivers the sufferer from suffering with futility. Our sufferings, when combined with the comforts that we have received from the 'God of all comfort'...(get this)...enable us to become agents of comfort to those around us who are caught in the currents of their own sufferings.

This transforming truth gives us a clue as to why the Lord Jesus allows His own very dear children to pass through various, sometimes painful, and often prolonged, trials. Such experiences open up avenues of ministry, which would otherwise be closed. If Christians walked only flower-strewn pathways of ease, the suffering world around them would be road-blocked to them. It is precisely because a believer has walked some sorrowful path, and discovered grace there in some new way, that he can relate to and minister to a fallen world around him. Understanding this delivers the suffering saint from the further pain of seeing their trial as futile. Trials in the life of a sanctified servant can be redeemed to become openings for ministry.

A message that cascades from this truth comes in the form of a warning: Christian! Don't waste trials! Allow them to drive you nearer and nearer to your Lord Jesus. Allow them to uproot you from the world and to re-plant you deep in the God of all comfort. A believer wastes his trials when he kicks against God while under them. They fail to do their good work in the saint's life if he complains against God rather than submitting to the Master's hand. Submit to the Lord in them. Pray and ask Him to make you a greater blessing to a hurting world because these trials have come upon you.

Believer, for all the joys of this life, for all of the sunny days given to us to enjoy, we are not offered a life totally free from the tribulations common to our fallen race. God has designed it this way so that we can reach into the suffering world around us with the comfort we have received. Praise God for His amazing work in and through our lives!

John Gillespie

Let no debt remain outstanding,
except the continuing debt to love one another,
for he who loves his fellow-man
has fulfilled the law.
Romans 13:8

Dear Church,

Take just a minute and chew on the scripture text at the top of this page. It is no news to you for me to tell you that we are hearing a lot these days about debt, and most of what we hear is pretty disheartening. We are hearing every day about bad debts, the debt crisis, debt consolidation, etc. etc. etc. People are putting themselves in impossible situations because they want to 'have it all'... now.

In particular I want us to focus on the form of debt described in the passage from Romans above. Notice that the Bible here clearly states that as Christians we are to faithfully pay off all earthly, financial debts: 'Let no debt remain outstanding...' But then notice that there is another form of debt, not financial, to which every Christian has an obligation:

'...the continuing debt to love one another'

I just want to highlight three things about this form of debt:

1. It is a reasonable obligation, for we are empowered by Jesus Christ to fulfil it. We do not seek to love one another in our own strength, through our own meagre resources, which would quickly be depleted. When we try to love in our own power, we run the risk of bankruptcy.

2. It is an ongoing obligation, for it is a continuing debt. With this world's debts you can pay them off, or default on them, or declare bankruptcy, but with the debt to love each other, we discover an ongoing debt that we can never pay off. We can never get to the place where we say, 'I have loved you enough... I can stop now... your turn.'

3. It is a universal obligation, for we are to love one another. Some are easier to love than others, but 'one another' sets no boundaries to our debt of love. 'One another' implies those we enjoy loving, and those who give us nothing in return. This requires an endless 'bank' from which we can draw, and that bank is Jesus Himself and His boundless store of grace.

Well, regardless of what the economy does, regardless of your personal financial blessings or woes, we are all in debt to one another, to love one another with the love of Jesus Christ. Let's seek grace (boundless grace!) to fulfil the 'unfulfillable'... our debt of love to those around us. Begin with your nearest neighbours... your spouse... and family... then move out to your church and community.

In so doing we will be a greater witness to the world than ever we could imagine.

Jesus said:

> *'By this all men will know that you are my disciples, if you love one another.'*

Grace and peace to you in all abundance through our Lord and Saviour Jesus Christ,

John Gillespie

O God, You are my God,
earnestly I seek You;
my soul thirsts for You,
my body longs for You,
in a dry and weary land
where there is no water.
Psalm 63:1

Dear Beloved in Christ,

I want to take a few minutes to encourage you in the good and Godly habit of developing a daily quiet time with the Lord Jesus.

I realise that many of you have for many years been spending time with the Lord Jesus most every, if not every, day, and have found the practice to be a life-line for your soul. May this offering of mine encourage you to continue on in your private time with the Lord.

But I am most concerned here to encourage and motivate those of us who have yet to establish a daily life-line with the Lord to 1) see the value in it and 2) to acquire the basic skills needed to have a helpful quiet time every day.

1) The Value of a Daily Quiet Time. I can put it this strongly: There is no substitute for a time each day with the Lord. Look at the verse at the top of this letter. Do you see the desperation in the Psalmist? He must meet with the Lord! He will rise early to spend time with his God. There is a thirst in his soul that only the Lord can satisfy. Personally, I cannot exist without a peaceful 'still point' with my Saviour every day. He is my Source and my Strength and I cannot do without time with Him.

I am praying that God will make us all desperate for Him.

The Lord Jesus, God the Son, was desperate for time with His Heavenly Father. Want proof? Have a look: Very early in the morning, while it was still dark, Jesus got up, left the house and went off to a solitary place, where he prayed. Mark 1:35 . Now, if the Lord Jesus needed a dedicated prayer time, what does that say about you and me?

2) Helpful Keys to a Successful Quiet Time. What I am going to share now is not 'rocket science'... it is more important than that. But these keys are not difficult to grasp and they will help you.

Discipline your sleep habits (yes, I really mean this!). If meeting with Jesus is important enough to you, than try going to bed early enough to allow you to rise early enough to give you time to meet with the Lord Jesus before the start of your busy day. Don't try to burn the candle at both ends (the Bible warns that this is a vain practice, Ps 127:2). Retire a bit earlier in the night because you have an appointment with the maker of the universe in the morning.

Truly believe that the Lord Himself will address you personally through His Word. I believe that the Bible shows me Christ and reveals God's mind to me when I prayerfully read it. If you are not sure where to begin, I suggest a chapter of Mark's Gospel every morning, and a section of Psalm 119. When you read it, ask the Holy Spirit to illuminate it to you. Seek to discover a new facet of Jesus Christ, what He is like, and how He acts. See what insights you can gain into what it will mean for you to trust and follow Christ today.

Take a few minutes to pray over your day. Bring your family to Christ in prayer. Pray for their protection from sin and Satan. Pray for your church, pastor, community group. As you develop your 'muscles', your quiet time prayer list will undoubtedly grow.

Finally, take a few minutes and worship the Lord. Thank Him for His grace. Reflect upon what you have learned in your Scripture reading. Deliberately open your heart to Him and ask Him to be your joy and strength for the day ahead.

The above may take only twenty minutes, especially at the start. But it can become a life-changing part of your day that will grow and develop in richness and depth.

John Gillespie

DON'T GIVE UP!

Dear Family,

Tessa and I are reading Jonathan Aitken's biography of John Newton together. We are being much encouraged by the amazing story of the man who wrote, among other hymns, 'Amazing Grace'.

What is most amazing to us is the tracking of the work of God's grace over the course of Newton's life... from slave trader to saint. This guy was bad... really bad. Even the other slavers couldn't stand him. His conversion came very gradually. There seemed to be a number of 'false starts' when an apparent work of grace would take place in his heart, but then Newton would go back to his 'old ways'.

Most of us would have written him off... but not Jesus Christ. The Lord Jesus had John Newton in His sights, and for Newton there would finally be no escaping God's 'Amazing Grace'.

Now what I find so encouraging about this is that his life was and still is a real testimony of the dogged perseverance of the Lord in the saving of a wayward soul. Some, a few, a precious few, have a 'Damascus Road' experience whereby their conversion is so radical and complete that they seem to never really look back or wander away again. But for many of us, and for many of those for whom we are longing and praying, the road to final conversion seems much more twisted and tortuous. Some for whom we are praying and hoping seem to have one false beginning after another... a good season followed by yet another foray into the 'world'. The 'old ways' just seem to have such a grip on them.

How many mothers are sighing out endless prayers for a wayward child? Who can count the tears of a father as he watches his dear child wander still farther into the darkness? How many spouses are longing and waiting for the conversion of an unbelieving partner? How many faithful friends are looking year in year out for God to do a saving work in the life of their companion?

If you have a wayward loved one or friend for whom you have been praying and longing for their soul's salvation, I want you to take great encouragement from the life of John Newton. Some souls are hard to save! But God is able! Don't give up! Keep on praying, hoping, believing. Keep right on taking every God-given opportunity to share the Good News of Jesus Christ. Keep seeking to live a winsome life that the beauty of Christ may be seen even through you. Don't be discouraged by the false starts and relapses. God is able to conquer the toughest soul. In my (now many) years as a pastor, I have seen many 'John Newtons'... weary and wayward souls who seem to walk in good ways with the Lord, and then... Oh! Old habits and haunts come calling and... back to the darkness they go. BUT God will have the last Word, and His grace is sufficient to open the most stubborn, lost and worldly hearts. He can make a trophy of grace out of a tragic life.

As long as there is a God of grace ruling this Universe there is hope for the John Newtons of this world.

Keep praying,
Witnessing,
Believing.

DON'T GIVE UP!

John Gillespie

HOW CAN I DISCOVER GOD'S WILL FOR MY LIFE?

Dear Friends,

One of the most frequently asked questions which I am asked in my pastor's study is: 'How can I discover God's will for my life?'

This simple but vexing question is of profound importance for all followers of Jesus Christ, not only for those in their teens and early twenties, but for all disciples at every stage of life.

Now, I don't want to underestimate the gravity of the question, or to over-simplify the way towards a sure answer, but I really do believe that there is a 'formula' for discovering the will of God in our lives that is all but failure-proof. I am going to give you the formula, then show you the scripture from which it is derived, and then encourage you to apply it in your life.

Here is the 'formula':

Worship – Worldliness + God's Word = Discovery of God's Will

Here's the scripture:

Therefore, I urge you brothers, in view of God's mercy, to offer your bodies as living sacrifices, holy and pleasing to God – this is your spiritual service of worship. Do not conform any longer to the pattern of this world, but be transformed by the renewing of your mind. Then you will be able to test and approve what God's will is – His good, pleasing and perfect will. (Romans 12: 1-2).

Now, if you take a careful look at the passage above, you will see the 'equation' or 'formula' very clearly in it. Go ahead and take some time right now to hunt for it...

...Do you see it?

...It really is very clear, and makes great sense.

Just in case you haven't found it, let me help you.

In the passage, written by the Apostle Paul to the Christians in Rome, Paul is urging the Roman Christians to respond to the wonders of the Gospel:

Therefore, in view of God's mercy...

1) Offer your bodies in living sacrifice to God – this is your spiritual act of worship.

Here is the first part of the equation... Worship: The offering of our living selves to God, not holding anything back, not striking any bargains, but placing ourselves and our lives every day on the altar of worship as a lifestyle. So we have:

Worship

2) Do not conform any longer to the pattern of this world.

Here is the next part of the formula: Refuse to be shaped by the values of the world around you. Literally 'do not let the world squeeze you into its mould'. Say 'no' to the self-centred, me-first values of a fallen society. Now we have:

Worship – Worldliness

3) But be transformed by the renewing of your mind.

Next... allow God's Word to have its way in reshaping you from the core out. Get your mind thinking the way God thinks by getting His Word into you. So now we have:

Worship – Worldliness + God's World

4) Then we will be: Able to discover God's will. His wonderful (good), satisfying (pleasing) and fulfilling (perfect) will.

See it?

Worship – Worldliness + God's Word = Discovery of God's Will

Now, each part of the equation is of vital importance! You cannot change the formula. For instance, if you want to discover God's will (wanting the joy and fulfilment which comes from being where God wants you to be), but refuse to 'present your body as a living sacrifice' (Worship), insisting on living for yourself instead of Christ, the formula falls apart. If you want to be in the centre of God's will, but also insist on holding to your worldly values of 'me first' (worldliness), the equation simply won't add up.

So! There you have it: a straightforward answer to an age old question... clear as it can be and right there in the Bible. God has a will for each of our lives, a purpose that fits us, a reason to live that fulfils us and gives Him glory. Plug your life into the equation, and... dare I say... I guarantee that you will discover your very purpose for living this year... and beyond. There is no other reasonable response to the Jesus Christ for a believer.

Oh, by the way, it works for families and churches too!

Let's do it together!

Yours,

John Gillespie

Dear Brothers and Sisters in Christ,

In case you have never noticed, I value and cherish the Bible as God's Word almost above anything else on earth. I would choose a Bible over any earthly possession. I want to tell you why.

God speaks to me through His perfect Word. I really believe that. In a world of a thousand voices all calling for and demanding my attention, I believe that the God of Eternity addresses me personally, and the Church collectively, through the Book of books, the Bible. When I take time to open God's book, and when I humbly ask the Holy Spirit to shine upon the sacred page, God speaks to me through the written word as surely as if He were sitting next to me. He shows me Jesus Christ in His Word. He feeds my soul through His Word. He chastens, comforts, and guides me through His Word.

Indeed, I understand the sentiments of the Psalmist, who, when speaking of God's written Word, said:

Your word is a lamp to my feet and a light to my path. (Psalm 119:105)

and

The unfolding of your words gives light; it gives understanding to the simple. (Psalm 119:130)

The Bible is for me a sure Word, an inexhaustible mine of treasure that ministers Jesus Christ to my mind and soul day in and day out, year in and year out.

Now, I know that the Bible has taken its knocks through the centuries, but it simply does not stay on the canvas. It keeps getting on its feet again, and is never down and out for the count. One of the great (but not good) Emperors of Rome (I think it was Julian) said 'destroy those Christians... and their book!' He was not able to do either, nor has anyone else since, nor will anyone hence.

One of the great challenges to the Bible today, however, is coming from right within the camp. It is not the Roman Emperor, or some boasting atheist who is launching the greatest and most dangerous attack on the Word of God. I fear that the greatest and most dangerous attack may well be arising from those who, one would believe, would be the most passionate about the Word of God. The attack is most sinister in its subtlety.

Perhaps there is nothing so threatening to the life of the Word of God in the midst of the people of God as the growing neglect of the Bible among those who claim to be believing followers of Jesus Christ... US. Now, here is a truly strange situation: a people who claim to be hungry for the Lord (or so we say in our songs), and who long for intimacy with Jesus Christ (or so we say in our prayers), who want guidance in life so as to do the will of God (or so we say to one another), but who can and often do go days or more at a time with our Bibles closed and collecting dust in some forgotten corner of our lives and homes. And then, just to add a bit more irony, some of us will long for some 'word from the Lord' from another source.

Let me finish the warning, and then get back to encouraging. To expect God to speak to us while we neglect His Word is pure presumption. To expect genuine intimacy with the Christ of time and eternity (and not some invented idol of our own fanciful imaginations) while our Bibles sit closed under a stack of magazines, is wishing for the impossible. Christians who marginalize the Bible in their daily lives do more to endanger their species than the tyrants of Rome and their successors could ever do. When we claim to be Bible believers but live to a large degree in daily neglect of God's precious Word, we do more to marginalise God's Truth in society than someone like Richard Dawkins and his merry band of atheists ever will.

We need to cherish God's Word if we expect to survive. We need to cherish God's Word if we expect God's Word to have influence in the society around us.

And His Word is worth cherishing! Countless millions of simple believers, over twenty centuries, and in every corner of the world can testify to the sufficiency of the Bible to bring them into a rich, growing, life-transforming relationship with the living God.

Pray and ask God to give you a new hunger for the Bible.

Stretch yourself and start memorizing scriptures.

Seek to be diligent in a daily quiet time with the Lord.

Read the Bible to your family.

Ask God to show you Jesus Christ in the scriptures.
Rediscover what GOD can do in your life through His wonderful Word.

One last thing: I and my colleagues are committed to being Bible men.

We have no other calling than to minister Jesus Christ to you from the pages of the Scriptures...

PLEASE PRAY FOR US AS WE SEEK TO BE FAITHFUL SERVANTS OF GOD'S WORD.

John Gillespie

GUARANTEES FOR BELIEVERS

Dear family,

I feel I need to bring a little clarification to something that I emphasised from the pulpit last Sunday morning.

You may recall that I said that the only thing that I can guarantee you as your pastor is deliverance from the wrath of God through the power of the shed blood of Christ. I cannot guarantee you health, financial advancement, temporal success, etc.

Now, for the most part, I really do stand by that statement.

Overall, I think it is true. I think its truth is found everywhere in the scriptures. Believers who have been truly delivered from the righteous wrath of God through the blood of His Son, do not always fare well here on Earth. There is not only no guarantee that they will always fare well, there are actually many promises that suffering and hardship await true believers this side of Heaven. God is not a salesman who only tells us what we want to hear. He tells us the truth even down to the 'fine print', and the Bible makes the reality of persecution and trials for God's children abundantly plain. I could provide many scriptures to prove my point, but I think you already agree with me, and some of those scriptures are probably already coming to your minds.

But, there are some other wonderful things that God guarantees to us, and we should not fail to be mindful of such things.

He promises His presence with us always:

'Never will I leave you; never will I forsake you.' So we say with confidence, 'The Lord is my helper; I will not be afraid. What can man do to me?' (Heb 13:5-6)

He promises sufficient grace for all circumstances:

'My grace is sufficient for you, for my power is made perfect in weakness.' (2 Cor 12:9)

He promises to change us and to not give up the project until we are holy:

[H]e who began a good work in you will carry it on to completion until the day of Christ Jesus. (Phil 1:6)

And you may bring to mind other guarantees in which believers can and should rejoice. But we should bear in mind that all these other guarantees are in place because we have been delivered from God's wrath, saved and sealed, by the blood of Christ. That is the wellspring from which all other blessings flow. Hence, Paul says:
He who did not spare His own Son, but gave Him up for us all – how will He not also, along with Him, graciously give us all things? (Romans 8:32)

But, furthermore, there are many, many blessings in this Christian life which, while not being 'guaranteed' in the same sense of our salvation through Christ, (that is, absolutely, sure, by virtue of the blood of Christ, and received without question by a simple act of faith) are nevertheless there for us in Christ to believe in, and fight in faith for. We will impoverish ourselves if we fail to see the many precious promises that God has for us as His children.

For example:

God promises to meet all our needs:

And my God will meet all your needs according to his glorious riches in Christ Jesus. (Phil. 4:19)

God invites us to pray in faith for impossible situations and believe for great results:

Now to him who is able to do immeasurably more than all we ask or imagine, according to his power that is at work within us. (Eph. 3:20)

God wills for us to pray in faith for the sick and ask in faith for their healing:#

Is any one of you sick?

He should call the elders of the church to pray over him and anoint him with oil in the name of the Lord. And the prayer offered in faith will make the sick person well; the Lord will raise him up. If he has sinned, he will be forgiven. (Jas 5:14,15)

God offers us joy and abundance in life through Jesus Christ:

'I have come that they might have life, and have it to the full.' (John 10:10)

And, again, there are many other very precious promises in the Word of God for us to rejoice in, receive, and act upon. Yes some 'health and wealth' teachers have abused such promises in order to feed their (and our) greed and lust, but that does not mean that we should not benefit from the abundance offered us in God's Word as His children.

As we live under the great guarantee of deliverance from wrath through the blood of Jesus Christ, please lets be encouraged to 'press in' with the very many and precious promises of God for His Church. How tragic if we live like paupers when God wills us to live as sons of the King! May the Lord lead us to new frontiers of faith where we are trusting Him in new ways, and in new areas. With eyes fixed confidently on eternity, lets live boldly by faith during our brief sojourn here in time.

Yours, for Christ's glory

John Gillespie

I know that praying for the sick is challenging to faith, and often raises many questions regarding God's sovereignty, but I am happily committed to this ministry because 1) God encourages it and 2) God never fails to bring blessing to the saints and glory to Himself even if He deems it right to heal through death or give grace for prolonged suffering. Such an attitude toward God's sovereignty does not reflect a 'cop out' by those who hold it, but a deep confidence (faith) in the character of God.

THE JOB IS STILL THERE TO DO

Dear Brothers and Sisters,

I want to take just a few minutes of your time to reflect upon our journey together as a family of churches, and to point our sights outward towards the fields around us that are ready for harvest.

For the Gillespie family, this August will mark the beginning of our twenty-third year here in Southeast Cornwall. Without any question we have seen the goodness of the Lord in the establishment of what we are coming to see not as just one wonderful church at Morval, but of a growing family of churches right here in our corner of Cornwall. Together there have been many battles, not a few disappointments, plenty of tears, hours of prayer, and a firm faith that the Bible brings life to desert places. How Tessa and I praise God for all of you who over the years have lived faithfully for Christ and have encouraged us in our service with you.

I hope we all realize that what we have here is very precious. It is no small thing to see Jesus Christ build His church right before our eyes. So many dear believers live out their lives seeing nothing but decline and retreat. We all are being privileged to see joyful advance and growth. Of course we realize that things are not perfect. But they are good. And Jesus Christ is with us!

If we each began to recall names of those who have gone before us in this work, those in glory now, those now serving in far off places who were first encouraged to follow Christ or to consider deeper service right here among us, we will have even greater reason to praise Jesus!

But (there is always a 'But', isn't there?)... the job is so far from finished. I think of Winston Churchill's observation after an early decisive victory in the War: 'This is not the end... or even the beginning of the end... this is the end of the beginning.' And I think that is where we are. We are at the 'end of the beginning'. We have seen three Bible-based, Christ-centred, people-loving churches established. These are mission stations not clubhouses! It is from these churches that Christ-exalting ministry at home and abroad is to be launched. It is imperative that we keep this perspective in mind.

Let's hear a bit of humbling news... our communities are still largely ignorant of the Gospel, gleeful to be living in a 'post-Christian' age, and do not believe that Jesus Christ and His truth are a force to be reckoned with. They largely ignore us as a Church and, worse, ignore our precious Lord and Saviour, Jesus Christ. The job is still there to do!

So, there is every reason to be thankful, and every reason to be diligent in our witness and evangelism. Pray and ask the Lord for dreams and visions of how He can use you and us in the greatest work of all: the spreading of His fame.

The BEST is ahead!

'My food,' said Jesus, 'is to do the will of Him who sent me and to finish his work. Do you not say, "Four months more and then the harvest"? I tell you, open your eyes and look at the fields! They are ripe for harvest. Even now the reaper draws his wages, even now he harvests the crop for eternal life, so that the sower and the reaper may be glad together.

'Thus the saying "One sows and another reaps" is true. I sent you to reap what you have not worked for. Others have done the hard work, and you have reaped the benefits of their labour.'
(John 4:34-38)

Yours for Him,

John Gillespie

Dear Church,

Having been privileged to be a pastor now for more than a quarter of a century, I can confidently say that virtually all problems in church life fall into one of the following two categories:

> *1) Doctrinal problems*
> *2) Relational problems*

Here in the GCC Family we are, thankfully, free from most doctrinal problems... we tend to believe the right things.

> *BUT... we are not immune from relational problems.*

Be sure of this: Satan can undo a Church as certainly through strife between brothers and sisters as he can through heresy. I have spent countless hours lamenting unforgiveness between brothers and sisters. We have cried rivers of tears over fractured relationships. God's work has often been brought to a grinding halt through misunderstanding, pride, hardness of heart towards another for whom Christ died, or via good old fashioned, Satan-glorifying unforgiveness.

Getting along with one another is not an option for those of us in the Body of Christ. It is a direct command from Headquarters. Consider the following scriptures:

Therefore, if you are offering your gift at the altar and there remember that your brother has something against you, leave your gift there in front of the altar. First go and be reconciled to your brother; then come and offer your gift. (Matt 5:23-24)

My command is this: Love each other as I have loved you. (Jn 15:12)

See to it that no one misses the grace of God and that no bitter root grows up to cause trouble and defile many. (Heb 12:15)

I could multiply Bible passages on this most vital theme, filling pages. You can discover them for yourself. The point is obvious and unavoidable: The Body of Christ travels on a road of Relationships. We cannot fail to 'seek peace and pursue it' (1 Peter 3:11). When relationships are undervalued, or allowed to collapse, the entire journey of the Church is jeopardized.

It is no use saying 'it's the other guy's fault'. God calls each of us to be 'peacemakers'.

It is no use excusing the rift as a mere 'private matter' between 'private parties'. In a body there are no private matters.

When we let the sun go down on our anger, we give the Devil a foothold (Eph 4:27). When we work hard for good relationships and forgive quickly, we give Satan little room to work.

I have very little fear that the evil one will get into our midst through heresy from our pulpits or community groups. Our teaching is pretty sound.

But...

Let us not be so foolish as to think he will not try another tactic to side-track this great work! Let's not even give him a chance!

When we fail to honour one another
   serve one another
     love one another
       forgive one another
         seek out fellowship with one another
           repent to one another
              cherish one another

we do the Devil's work... just as certainly as if I or another stands in the pulpit and proclaims heresy.

Now let's make it positive:

When we honour one another
serve one another
love one another
forgive one another
seek out fellowship with one another
repent to one another
cherish one another

we do Christ's work... just as certainly as if I or another stands in the pulpit and proclaims God's glorious truth.

Finally, before I close read below the wonderful words of Psalm 133. The blessings of unity are plain to see.

How good and how pleasant it is when brothers live together in unity! It is like precious oil poured on the head, running down on the beard, running down on Aaron's beard, down upon the collar of his robes. It is as if the dew of Hermon were falling on Mount Zion. For there the LORD bestows his blessing, even life for evermore.

Let the words sink in... and determine to live in harmony with your brothers and sisters.

Grace and Peace to all of you,

John Gillespie.

THE CLOCKMAKER

Dear Church Family,

In a small factory town in Bavaria there once lived a clockmaker. In his shop's front window, facing the town's Fore Street, stood the grandfather's clock which he had made years before when apprenticing for his trade.

Every day workmen bustled past his shop on their way to and from work in the factory.

Over time, the watchmaker began to notice that each and every morning a particular man, better dressed than those rushing to work alongside him, would stop and set his pocket watch to the time on the old grandfather's clock in the window. Days and weeks went by and the months turned into years. Every day the well-dressed man stopped to go through his time-keeping routine.

Finally the old watchmaker ventured outside to enquire of the man, 'Say there! Every day I see you stopping by my shop to set your pocket watch by my clock in the window. Why? What's your purpose in needing to be so exact?'

'Well', said the well-dressed man, 'You see, I am the manager at the factory, and among other things, it is my job to blow the whistle every day at precisely 5pm to signal an end to the work day. The whole town relies on that whistle being accurate. This old pocket watch of mine never has kept good time... and I rely on your fine clock to give me the correct time. Thanks to your clock I can blow the all-important whistle on time!'

'Oh dear,' said the red-faced old clockmaker, 'we have a problem! You see, that old grandfather's clock you rely on has never kept good time either. Every day I set its time by your factory whistle!'

The little story above illustrates very well the results of living without an absolute from which to measure all other areas of life. We can't live without standards, and we cannot have standards without a standard from which to judge and weigh all else.

PROBLEM: We live in an age that eschews any notion of absolute truth from which we can judge right and wrong and to which we can appeal. The last verse of the ancient book of Judges pretty well sums up our age:

'In those days there was no king in the land... everyone did as he saw fit in his own eyes.' (Judges 23:25)

In ancient Israel Relativism ruled and chaos flourished! So it seems to be in our day. When there is no 'king', that is, no agreed standard of judgement, everyone is left to be their own little king, that is, to determine truth as it suits them, to formulate standards that fit their own desires.

But the very freedoms we so cherish are built upon an agreed understanding that there is a higher law, above us, outside of us, whose origin is in the character of God Himself, from which we derive our values and make our choices, and to which we are all accountable. The freedom to live free from tyranny, to govern oneself, is entirely dependent upon a common conviction that there is Absolute Truth that ultimately sits in judgement above us all. But if the clockmaker's clock keeps time badly, then all the pocket watches in town are set to the wrong time! Anarchy rules where Truth doesn't!

Over the past generation, we have watched our lawmakers steadily overthrow laws that were founded upon the common belief that there was a God from whom all true law comes. We have allowed our schools and universities to teach our young minds that 'there is no such thing as absolute truth' (that popular claim contradicts itself... can you see how?). We ourselves have often marginalised God and His Truth, in favour of our own self interests. The Church has often been no more faithful in keeping a plumb line for Truth in society than was that old clockmaker's clock faithful in setting a reliable time for the town to run by.

Beloved, if our society is to survive, then the Church (that's you and me!) needs to believe and declare to our 'kingless' generation that there is a King. There is Truth (with a capital 'T'). There is a God who speaks, and feels, and hears, and sees, and saves, and judges. This is our calling and our charge. We need to live under the Lordship of Christ ourselves, and then call our generation to live under His Lordship with us. The only other option will be the destruction of society as we know it, and the loss of our very freedom, so rare and once cherished.

Pray and ask the Lord to give you fresh courage to live under the wonderful Lordship of Jesus Christ, that we together might make choices and cherish values that reflect His Truth. Flee moral compromise, and avoid the temptation to 'fit in' to a world that refuses to acknowledge that there is a God of Truth who governs all things. Ask God for a new courage to witness to a rudderless world.

There is no other hope for our world than the Truth that is in Jesus Christ.

John Gillespie

FAMILIES – THE TOUGH MISSION FIELDS

*'Go home to your family and tell them how much the Lord
has done for you, and how He has had mercy on you.'*

Dear Church Family,

The words above were spoken by the Lord Jesus to a man from whom He had just delivered a whole host of demons. You can read about the entire event in Mark, chapter 5.

Having just been set free from forces that had controlled his life, perhaps for all of his life, he understandably wanted to follow Jesus from henceforth wherever Jesus went. But Jesus would not let him. Instead, he told him to do something that is arguably the toughest assignment in the Christian life: To 'go home to your family and tell them how much the Lord has done for you, and how He has had mercy on you.'

I think we will all admit that our families are perhaps the toughest mission fields of all. They know all about us! They have seen us at our worst. What a task Jesus assigns this newly converted, freshly delivered man! Could he not go to Bible School first with Jesus and the disciples and then, a few years down the road, perhaps after founding some great ministry (i.e. 'Demoniacs Anonymous'), achieving some fame, proving himself, go and give the Gospel in power to Mum and Dad?

No, Jesus sent him straight away, with nothing but the power of his testimony of God's grace in his life. Notice what Jesus did not tell him to say or do:

Go home and:
Impress them with how much Bible knowledge you now have...
Amaze them with your new found super-spirituality...

Tell them they are all going to hell if they do not become like you...
Promise them that you'll never mess up again...

No, the assignment was simple and fool-proof:

Go home and tell...

What the Lord has done for you. How He has had mercy on you.

In other words... give them your testimony, but make it a Christ-centred testimony. Tell of God's goodness to your needy soul. Speak of God's grace to a ruined man. There is perhaps little so powerful as a testimony of God's grace. It can even work on family members!

I am sometimes concerned that when we have new encounters with the Lord, perhaps at a conference, or some such event, we develop a sense of spiritual superiority. The last thing we have in mind is our family, or perhaps our Church family. We want to leave such stragglers behind and move on in a new circle of spiritual experience. But the Lord Jesus may not want us to do that! He may say to us just what he said to the delivered man! 'Go home' (back to your kindred, or back to your local church). 'Bless others by telling of My goodness to you.' 'Speak not of their inadequacy, but of My mercy.' 'See what I can do through you in the toughest mission field of all... your own back yard!'

What was the result of this man's return to his home town?

'The man began to tell how much Jesus had done for him...
And all the people were amazed.'

Let's live for the fame of Christ, even with our families, church families and friends.

Grace and Peace,

John Gillespie

'Come to me, all you who are
weary and burdened,
and I will give you rest.'
Matthew 11:28

For more information on our churches go to

www.graceccmorval.co.uk
www.torpointcc.org.uk
www.bodmincommunitychurch.com

*A selection of John Gillespie's sermons
are available online,
see* www.graceccmorval.co.uk
The sermons are also available on CD

For more information contact the church office as follows:

Grace Community Church
Oak Trees
Morval
Looe
Cornwall
PL13 1PR

Church Office telephone 01503 240930
Mon - Fri - 09.30 - 12.30